# The Peace Corps and More

## 175 WAYS TO WORK, STUDY AND TRAVEL AT HOME & ABROAD

by Medea Benjamin
and Miya Rodolfo-Sioson

A Project of Global Exchange

**Library of Congress Cataloging-in-Publication Data**
   The Peace Corps and More: 175 Ways to Work, Study and Travel at Home and Abroad by Medea Benjamin and Miya Rodolfo-Sioson
   p. cm.
   Includes bibliographic references and index.
   ISBN 0-929765-04-4
   1. Peace Corps (U.S.) 2. Non-governmental organizations - Developing countries - Directories. I. Benjamin, Medea, 1952-. II. Rodolfo-Sioson, Miya.
   HC60.5.B46 1997
   361.6-dc20                  90-27827
                                                    CIP

Cover design: Lindsay Anderson
Page Design and Layout: Kevin Danaher
Printing: McNaughton & Gunn
Published by Global Exchange

10 9 8 7 6 5 4 3

**Acknowledgments**
Many thanks to Derrick Ong for his help in researching the third edition of this book. We would also like to thank Renato Rodolfo-Sioson for editing assistance.

*We need your help!* To make this guide as useful as possible, please let us know of any changes in organizations listed here and any new ones we should add. We'd like to hear about your experiences looking for an overseas placement, as well as your experiences abroad. Please keep in touch.

The Peace Corps and More
c/o Global Exchange
2017 Mission St., #303
San Francisco, CA 94110
(415) 255-7296
email: gx-info@globalexchange.org

# Table of Contents

**Photo credits**
pp. 6, 72, and 82 ... Adam Kufeld
p. 15 ... World Bank Photo
p. 23 ... Liz Chilsen
p. 93 ... Jean Weisinger
p. 110 ... Gayle Smith
cover... P. Johnson

# What Is Global Exchange?

Global Exchange is a nonprofit research, education and action center building people-to-people ties between countries in the North and countries in the South (also known as the "Third World"). Through these linkages, we find ways in which citizens of different nations can work together to combat poverty, environmental destruction and war. Our programs include:

• **Reality Tours.** Global Exchange sponsors tours all over the world—tours that provide visitors with a true understanding of a country's internal dynamics. Get beyond the beaches, resort hotels, and souvenir shops, and into the villages and homes of local people. Learn about some of the most pressing issues confronting the world, and have fun too!

Global Exchange sponsors many different types of trips, from human rights delegations to environmental trips, women's delegations and family vacations. We are the only U.S.-based organization sending monthly study seminars to Cuba. We organize work/study opportunities in Mexico, where the profits go to support the local health clinic; fact-finding delegations to South Africa and Haiti; and fascinating trips to California farms to compare chemical-intensive agriculture with organic farming.

These tours help us break down barriers and harmful stereotypes and replace them with strong bonds of compassion and friendship.

• **Partnerships with Grassroots Organizations.** Global Exchange is not a wealthy organization. But we have discovered that small amounts of money, supplies, and technical assistance—given to the right groups at the right times—can make a huge difference.

Our help in building and equipping a health clinic in Honduras has meant that thousands of poor Hondurans now have access to health care. In Haiti, we fund a rural group that improves the agricultural skills of poor peasants, putting more food on their tables. In Vietnam, we provide scholarships to poor rural women so that they can continue their education. And in our home base in San Francisco, we sponsor a cultural center for inner city youth, where they learn skills to earn a dignified living.

Through these partnerships, we have formed strong bonds with community organizers, environmental activists, and human rights advocates throughout the world.

• **Fair Trade.** To help build economic justice from the bottom up, Global Exchange promotes what we call "fair trade"—trade that directly benefits the producers. We support hundreds of artisans by selling their crafts at our Third World Crafts Centers in San Francisco and Berkeley, and at our art shows and fairs. Our stores also provide an excellent forum for educating North Americans about Third World realities.

Global Exchange is also actively involved in strengthening the North American Alternative Trading Organization, an umbrella group for U.S. retailers and wholesalers concerned about providing producers with a fair income.

• **Public Education.** Global Exchange brings expert speakers to address schools, churches, and community centers around the country on topics such as world hunger, grassroots development, U.S. foreign policy, environmentalism, and human rights. Speakers have included Honduran peasant activist Elvia Alvarado, Haitian lawyer and educator Claudette Werleigh, and South African religious leader Sister Bernard Ncube.

We offer a wide range of resources—books, videos, resource guides, fact sheets—to help explain the roots of social and environmental problems and to encourage people to get actively involved. Our books *Bridging the Global Gap: A Handbook to Linking Citizens of the First and Third Worlds, Corporations Are Gonna Get Your Mama: Globalization and the Downsizing of the American Dream* and *50 Years Is Enough: The Case Against the World Bank and the International Monetary Fund* are invaluable tools for activists.

We urge you to become a member of Global Exchange. With your annual membership contribution of $35 or more ($25 for low income), you will receive our quarterly newsletter that keeps you up-to-date on key issues in the internationalist movement. You will also receive a full list of our "Reality Tours" and priority consideration on those tours, as well as a 10% discount on our educational resources and Third World crafts.

Please fill out the membership coupon at the back of this book. We thank you in advance for your generous support!

# 1
# CHECK OUT
# YOUR OPTIONS

How can U.S. citizens learn more about Third World realities while at the same time contributing to the struggle for social justice? We at Global Exchange are constantly asked this question by socially and environmentally conscious people who want to work overseas in a way that is consistent with their beliefs. This guide is our response. It offers a wide variety of Third World options—from building houses in Bangladesh, to protecting human rights in Guatemala, to staffing a health clinic in Mozambique.

But before you consider going to the Third World, it's crucial to clarify your motives. If you are interested in overseas work because you feel you have certain skills and ideas that can help improve the lives of poor people, you may be sorely disappointed.

There is an oft-told example of a Peace Corps volunteer who tried to improve the irrigation system in his assigned area. He noticed that the hand-operated device used to pump water took considerable time and effort to use. He therefore took the initiative to design and build a more efficient pump out of a bicycle that only needed someone to sit on the seat and pedal. But he failed to take into account that women were responsible for pumping water, and religious custom prohibited women from straddling a bicycle. The new, "efficient" pump went unused. As the story suggests, development is not something that can be attained by simply importing foreign technology and "know-how."

Another problem with foreigners is that they usually have book-learning but little practical experience. I have often seen young Americans in Africa, fresh out of U.S. agricultural schools, trying to teach farming to old-timers—men and women who know the terrain, know the climate, and have centuries of farming in their blood. This doesn't mean that African farmers can't benefit from new techniques, but it does mean that it will take someone with lots of practical experience and understanding of local conditions to teach them something truly beneficial.

Moreover, when North Americans travel abroad to "help" the poor, they often discover that the causes of poverty are very different—and more complex—than they had believed. This was my own experience many years ago when I was sent, straight out of public health school, to teach nutrition to indigenous women in the mountains of Guatemala. I had plenty of book-knowledge but little practical experience. I gathered the women together to explain the signs of malnutrition and teach them how to feed their children a more balanced diet. The women, ever so polite, told me that they knew the difference between healthy and unhealthy children. Their problem was not lack of knowledge, it was a lack of land to grow their own food and lack of money to buy it. I soon discovered that there were much larger political and economic causes of poverty that no foreigner could solve.

Before getting involved in development work, it is essential to understand that development cannot be equated with new techniques or new "things"—it is not water pumps or latrines or clinics or schools or particular agricultural innovations. No. Real development is a process of empowering the poor so that they can organize and change their own lives. This is why the strengthening of grassroots organizations—organizations helping the rural and urban poor, mobilizing women, or dealing with environmental, human rights, or peace issues—is key to a development process that truly benefits the poor.

**Essentially a Learning Experience**

If development is indeed a process of empowering the poor, then foreigners can be of assistance in this process, but they shouldn't initiate or try to control it. No matter what their skills or access to resources, foreigners should remain "on tap," not on top.

In fact, if you are going to work overseas, you should see yourself more in the role of a student than a teacher. For your time volunteering in a poor community abroad can be the most profound learning experience of your life. You might learn a new language, a new way of communicating. You experience new foods, new smells, new sights. You discover the charms and complexities of another culture. You make lifelong friends.

Perhaps most importantly, seeing a different way of living makes you look differently at your own culture and your own way of life. Spending time in a village with no electricity makes you realize how much we have lost in a culture that revolves around a TV screen. Being part of a tightly-knit community makes you see the emptiness of lives focused on individualism and rampant consumerism. And seeing people who get by with so little teaches you how to "tread more lightly on the planet." Spending time overseas can become a profound opportunity to rethink your own values and priorities, and to gain a new sense of what it means to be human.

**The Different Ways to Go Overseas**
Most of the organizations listed in this directory are private, nonprofit groups. While a few of them receive some U.S. government assistance, the only government-sponsored program listed here is the Peace Corps.

The Peace Corps is the largest U.S. agency that sends volunteers overseas. The Peace Corps is attractive in that it provides volunteers with airfare, a monthly stipend, medical insurance, and in-country infrastructure to lean on in times of need. It also offers training in foreign languages, cross-cultural sensitivity training and technical skills. Most of the other agencies listed in this book are too small or financially strapped to match the services the Peace Corps provides to its volunteers.

There are, however, a few negatives about the Peace Corps. One, it has become highly competitive. Gone are the days when the Peace Corps was looking for well-rounded "generalists." Nowadays the Peace Corps wants skilled people and it is highly competitive—only about one in six applicants gets accepted.

Furthermore, the Peace Corps calls for a two-year commitment. This is terrific if you really want to get a good sense of another culture, but often people are not ready to make such a significant time commitment.

The Peace Corps is also problematic if you have a family you want to take along. Children are prohibited. If you are married and want to serve together, both people must qualify, and then you must wait until a country requests both skills at the same time, in the same location. Couples must therefore be very patient, and may well not receive a placement.

A final problem with the Peace Corps is that it is part of a government-to-government program. This has two implications: one, you represent the U.S. government and two, you are a guest of your host government. Now, these may not be very significant issues if you are in a country where both U.S. policy and the host government are decent. There are many countries where the U.S. govern-

9

ment has little involvement in their internal affairs. And often volunteers are sent to small villages and have no contact with even local government officials.

But what if you were sent to the largest Peace Corps site, Honduras, in the late 1980s, when the United States was waging war in Central America and using Honduras as its military outpost? The Peace Corps office in Tegucigalpa was bombed in 1989 by locals who opposed the presence of the U.S. military in their country and saw the huge Peace Corps contingent as part of the problem.

Or what if you are in a country where the government is corrupt, and this begins to affect your work because you are involved with a government agency and see all kinds of irregularities? Being a guest of the government, you are not supposed to rock the boat. Or what happens when the best grassroots organizations in the country are off-limits to the Peace Corps because they are opposed by the government? This may well be the case, since grassroots groups often come under attack from the government when they confront the entrenched power of local elites.

The Peace Corps recruiters handbook states that volunteers can ask not to go to certain countries if they have "political/philosophical objections to U.S. policy" in those countries. You could, therefore, ask not to be sent to a particular country. Of course, if you go to the recruiters with a list of 20 countries you refuse to serve in, they will undoubtedly write you off as a candidate.

So while you may exclude a few places you find particularly objectionable, if you are unwilling to be associated with U.S. foreign policy in general, or want to be free to speak out against any local corruption or mismanagement you might find, or if you're not willing to make a two-year commitment, or if you don't have a skill that the Peace Corps is looking for, then you may have to look elsewhere.

## Alternatives to the Peace Corps

In this guide, you will find a wide variety of groups that send people to work overseas. While we have not been able to individually screen every organization, we have tried our best to select groups that do not impose their ideas and projects on local communities, but work to address needs identified by those communities themselves. This is easier said than done. Far too many organizations continue to view local communities as "beneficiaries" rather than as initiators of any development process.

So we strongly suggest that if you are seriously considering working with any U.S. organizations overseas, you carefully scrutinize their philosophy and practice. Read all of their written materials, talk to them about your concerns, and ask for the phone numbers of a few former volunteers. It is essential that you feel completely comfortable with the organization that you will be representing overseas.

Also included in this guide are a number of religious organizations. We have tried to exclude those that see their main mission as one of proselytizing. We have seen much damage done by religious groups that give greater priority to promoting their denomination than to helping empower the local people. Many of the organizations listed here do not require that volunteers be of the same faith. The Mennonites and the Quakers (the American Friends Service Committee), for example, only ask that volunteers be committed to the principle of nonviolence. So even if you are not a religious believer, you still might feel comfortable being associated with some of these faith-based organizations.

In terms of skill level, this guide contains suggestions for both the highly skilled (doctors, engineers, architects) and those with a more general background. One health group, The Flying Samaritans, is looking for plastic surgeons, while another, Pastors for Peace, needs people to drive their trucks and vans from various cities in the U.S. to Mexico and Central America.

**Travel and Study Opportunities**

While there are hundreds of organizations that accept overseas volunteers, remember that there are thousands of people like yourself looking for such opportunities. Obviously, those who are most qualified and have previous overseas experience will get priority. For those with little or no overseas experience, study tours such as the ones organized by our group, Global Exchange, are an excellent way to get a feel for the Third World and to make initial contacts that can help you set up a longer-term placement. The tours listed in the section on "Socially-Responsible Travel" are also excellent for people who want to understand and experience Third World realities but can only be away from home for several weeks at a time.

Another possibility is to travel as a student. Many of the listings in the "Study Opportunities" section of this guide do not require you to be a student from a particular institution or even a full-time student. Living in the Third World as a student also allows you to avoid playing the role of the "foreign expert" who comes to teach the local people how to "develop" themselves.

**Going the Direct Route**

For those who are particularly adventurous, or who cannot get a placement through the other organizations listed in this guide, there is another route: that of making direct contact with groups overseas. Only do this if you are willing to make at least a six-month commitment, and only if you can finance your own stay (you might be able to get a free place to live, but you'd have to pay your own airfare and expenses).

How can you find these grassroots groups? If you can narrow down the country you want to work in and the kind of work you want to do, then you can contact U.S. organizations that fund grassroots development and get the names of a few good groups in that country. Try contacting institutions that get U.S. government funding, since one of their mandates is to deal with the public. For Latin America, contact the Inter-American Foundation at 901 N. Stuart St., 10th floor, Arlington, VA 22203, (703) 841-3800; for Africa, the African Development Foundation at 1400 I St. NW, Suite 1000, Washington, DC 20005, (202) 673-3916; and for Asia, The Asia Foundation at 465 California St., San Francisco, CA 94104, (415) 982-4640. If you are a supporter of a private development group (like Oxfam, the American Friends Service Committee, or any number of groups that are part of the umbrella organization Interaction), you can ask that organization for help. It is also a service that we at Global Exchange provide for our members.

Remember, the more specific you are, the better. If you write to the Inter-American Foundation for the names and addresses of a few women's organizations in Ecuador, you are much more likely to receive a response than if you say you are interested in working somewhere in Latin America and would like some ideas.

I must warn you that oftentimes if you write directly to grassroots groups, you won't hear back from them. Many groups are understaffed and have a hard time responding to correspondence, and mail service in many Third World countries is dismal. If you do hear back, the response may be negative because the group doesn't know who you are. (If you can volunteer with a U.S. group and get a recommendation from them, your chances are much better.)

But if you are really anxious to work overseas, you still have another option: getting on a plane and going. I can't tell you the number of people I've met who, frustrated by many rejections, just went to their country of choice and started asking around. And of all the people I know who have done this (myself included), the experience has been terrific. There's no substitute for firsthand contact, and there's no substitute for being in the right place at the right time.

I ended up working with a terrific Swedish development group in West Africa because I happened to be there when they were looking for a nutritionist. I have a friend who was concerned about hunger in Africa, couldn't get a job with a U.S. relief group, so got on a plane to Somalia and was hired immediately. I also have a friend who had no particular development skills, but she decided to fly to Costa Rica and try to find work there. She ended up knocking on the doors of a public school and offering to teach English. She was welcomed with open arms, found a place to stay with a Costa Rican family, and had a wonderful stay.

Once you get to a country, the opportunities somehow present themselves—especially if you are a lively, outgoing person. But it obviously takes a lot of guts to go to an unfamiliar country with no set plan. If, however, you are the adventurous type, you will probably have the time of your life.

**How Can You Finance Your Stay Overseas?**
One of the most difficult issues for people wanting to volunteer overseas is where to get funding. Those who have prior overseas experience and are highly skilled—such as doctors, nurses, and agronomists—will obviously have a much easier time getting paid positions. For people with little experience and less specialized skills, the possibility of landing a paid position is close to zero. Why should an organization pay an inexperienced foreigner when they

can pay a local person who would be much more familiar with the culture, speaks the language fluently, and would be much more inclined to stick around?

Moreover, the majority of the groups in this guide are relatively small, nonprofit organizations that can only afford to pay volunteers a small stipend. In fact, some of the best groups in this guide cannot afford to pay volunteers anything at all.

There are some funds available for studying in the Third World. In Chapter 7, "Getting More Information," you'll find a list of financial resources that may be of use in pursuing scholarship opportunities. Some "socially responsible" travel groups, such as Global Exchange, have partial scholarships for low-income and minority applicants.

But to be realistic, if you really want to work, study, or travel overseas, you will most likely have to start out by working in the U.S. and saving up some money to pay for your trip. Don't get discouraged. A few thousand dollars can go a long way in most Third World countries. In fact, it will probably be one of the least expensive—and most rewarding—learning experiences you can possibly have.

A few caveats are in order. Many of the smaller groups listed here are in constant flux and frequently change addresses and phone numbers, so be prepared to do some updating on your own. (We'd appreciate any updates you can send us.)

Another caveat is that if you are in a hurry to go somewhere, you may be sorely disappointed by the schedules of many of the groups listed. For the Peace Corps, for example, it takes from six months to a year between the time you fill out an application and the time you are sent overseas. Some groups only have volunteer openings once a year.

We at Global Exchange wish you the best of luck in your search for meaningful work overseas. Please let us know how this guide can be more useful in future editions. We'd also love to hear about your experiences abroad, so keep in touch!

Medea Benjamin
Director, Global Exchange

# 2
# PRACTICAL TIPS

W hen traveling to the Third World, you always have to be flexible and ready for a change in plans. But the more you prepare beforehand, the smoother your trip will be. The following are some practical tips to help you make the most of your experience.

**Passports, Visas, Vaccinations**

All travelers abroad should have a current passport. You must apply for a passport in person if you are applying for the first time, if you are renewing a passport issued over 11 years ago, or if you were under 18 when you got your last passport. You can apply at selected post offices, at federal or state courts of records, or at one of the State Department passport agencies in larger cities. You can renew your passport by mail, but you must submit your old passport (issued within the past 11 years).

Don't leave this until the last minute, for it could take up to a few months to process an application, particularly for new passports.

Visa requirements vary from country to country. Contact the nearest embassy or consulate of the country you intend to visit to find out about visa requirements and special travel restrictions. Some countries require an International Certificate of Vaccination, a card issued by the World Health Organization that documents which inoculations you received before departure.

You may want to carry other forms of identification, such as an International Student or Teacher Identity Card, or an International Youth Card. These documents can save money on transportation, lodging, and other facilities. Contact the Council on International Educational Exchange at 205 E. 42nd St., New York, NY 10017-5706, (212) 822-2695 or (888) COUNCIL, http://www.ciee.org/ for more information on these documents.

**Keeping Your Money and Documents Safe**

Traveler's checks are the safest way to carry your money, and are accepted in most places. American Express, Citicorp, Thomas Cook and Visa are the most widely accepted. Some poor Third World countries will not accept traveler's checks, so check with the country's embassy or consulate in the U.S. before you go. The same is true for credit cards. In some places, you may have no choice but to carry cash.

Take great care to keep your money and documents safe! If you're staying in a hotel, always take them with you when you go out or leave them in a safe if the hotel offers this service. The best way to carry your valuables is in a money belt or neck pouch worn inside your shirt. It is also a good idea to carry photocopies of your passport and traveler's check receipts to facilitate matters if you lose your documents.

You should find out if your insurance program covers you while you are abroad. It's important to have health and accident insurance should a problem arise. In addition, you may want to explore the possibilities for baggage and flight insurance.

**Air Fares**

Air fares vary greatly, depending on when you are flying and where you buy your ticket. Peak fares are in effect from June to August, and prices increase as the date of departure approaches. You can often find cheap air fares if you are willing to travel with some restrictions. Normally, the more restrictions that apply to a ticket, the cheaper it is. You can get information on bargain tickets by exploring the travel section of major newspapers such as the *New York Times, Los Angeles Times,* and *San Francisco Chronicle.*

Charter flights are often the cheapest option for travelers, although you should read the fine print when purchasing a ticket because they often have certain restrictions. For charter flights, you can try the toll-free number for Council Travel: (800) 226-8624. You might also want to check into courier flights, where you give the courier service your baggage allotment in exchange for getting a discount ticket. You'll have to travel light—with only a carry-on— but it might be worth the savings. For a list of courier flights, contact Travel Unlimited at P.O. Box 1058, Allston, MA 02134. A good overview of using courier flights is *The Air Courier's Handbook* (1995) by Jennifer Basye, Big City Books, 7047 Hidden Lane, Loomis, CA 95650.

**Receiving Mail**

It's possible to receive mail while abroad, even if you don't have an address. Most post offices accept letters addressed to you care of

"Poste Restante." You may have to pay a small fee to pick up your mail. If you have an American Express card or traveler's checks, you can have letters sent to an American Express office. Get a list of their offices abroad from American Express at (800) 327-2177.

## Packing

Anyone who has spent time traveling will tell you "pack light!" You cannot take their advice too seriously. Pack your bags and then walk up and down a flight of stairs or around your neighborhood. If you get tired, reconsider what you are bringing and try to pare it down to the bare minimum. Most airlines permit each traveler two bags, weighing under 70 pounds each, but be sure to check your airline's baggage allowances. If you are changing airlines along the way, check with both so you won't be stuck paying a hefty price for overweight luggage.

You can increase your comfort by finding out about weather conditions at the time of year you'll be traveling. You should also inquire about local dress codes. If people do not show their legs in the area you'll be visiting, you may want to consider bringing long skirts and light pants instead of shorts. You will be treated with greater respect if you make an effort to respect the customs of the people you're visiting.

You should not bring clothes that need special care or have a great deal of sentimental value, especially if you will be abroad for an extended period of time. You should select clothes with the knowledge that they may be lost or ruined during the course of your trip. You may also want to bring clothes that you can leave behind at the end of the trip; many people you will befriend would appreciate a gift of clothing, or it could be donated to a group that gives clothes to needy people. Leaving things behind not only benefits the recipients; you will make space in your bags for items you buy abroad.

## Political Instability

If the political situation of the country you will be visiting is unstable, you may want to check on the current situation before you leave. The Public Information Office at the U.S. Department of State (formerly the Bureau of Public Affairs), (202) 647-6575, can give you the numbers of overseas embassies. The Overseas Citizens'

Service (formerly the Citizens' Emergency Center), (202) 647-5226, gives information about recent travel advisories. But you should not automatically cancel your trip because of a travel advisory. During the 1980s the U.S. government often warned against travel to Nicaragua, yet hundreds of thousands of visitors traveled there with few problems.

## Giving Gifts

Giving gifts to people who show you hospitality is a nice idea, but it should be done with caution. Gift giving in a tightly knit community, such as a small village, can cause conflict within the village. If you shower one family with gifts, others may be envious.

On the other hand, you will undoubtedly encounter many local people who will open up their homes and hearts to you, and you will want to leave them something to show your appreciation and affection. Gifts that are often appreciated and are not bulky to carry include solar calculators, children's books and puzzles, scissors and small tools, pocket knives, pens and pencils, music cassettes, perfume and T-shirts.

All too often, foreigners promise to send things to local people—photos, money, gifts—and then fail to follow through. DON'T MAKE PROMISES YOU CAN'T KEEP! You will not only disappoint the people you meet, but will make them more wary of all foreigners in the future.

## Health Tips

It's a good idea to get a general checkup with both your doctor and dentist to make sure you are in good health before going overseas. Many Third World countries have poor health care systems, so take all the precautions you can.

If you have glasses or contact lenses you should bring along an extra pair, as it may be hard to find replacements while abroad. If you are bringing prescription medication along, you should bring enough to last during your time overseas. Make sure you carry prescription drugs in their correctly labeled containers so they can't be confused with illegal drugs.

Many of the health problems that plague travelers abroad can be prevented by avoiding certain foods and drinks. Find out immediately if the water is safe to drink or must first be boiled.

Several months before you leave you should check what vaccinations, if any, you need. Some shots require several rounds, so it's a good idea to set up a timetable several months before you leave.

The Center for Disease Control (CDC) in Atlanta gives travelers advice regarding what inoculations are necessary before departure, and what medications should be brought along. Call their International Travel Hotline, (404) 639-2572, for general information; or the "International Travelers Health Information" on their Voice Information System, (404) 639-1610, for listings on malaria, yellow fever and other diseases. The International Association of Medical Assistance to Travelers (IAMAT) at 417 Center St., Lewiston, NY 14092, (716) 754-4883 can also give advice regarding specific health problems and health care abroad.

There is a growing movement to open the world of travel, work and study abroad to people with disabilities. Contact Mobility International USA at P.O. Box 10767, Eugene, OR 97440 for information and publications regarding opportunities abroad for people with disabilities.

**Taking Photos**

Picture-taking can become a controversial issue in the Third World. Oftentimes, the allure of a beautiful photograph overtakes the need to be culturally sensitive, and even the most aware person runs the risk of offending people by taking their picture against their wishes. Many people do not like to have their picture taken for personal or religious reasons. Others may not mind if they are asked first, especially if they have some kind of relationship with the photographer. If in doubt, it's safer to not take the picture.

Please note also that taking photographs of religious structures like churches, mosques, and shrines (especially their interiors) is almost a universal taboo. Tourists have been beaten for violating this rule. First ask a local if you are unsure.

Another note of caution: Many countries do not permit people to photograph government buildings, harbors, airports, bridges, and military bases and personnel. Authorities who see a foreigner photographing sensitive sites may not hesitate to rip the entire roll of film from his or her camera or, worse yet, take them into custody.

## Preparing Yourself Mentally

Perhaps more important than getting your shots on time and visiting the dentist is preparing yourself mentally for a living situation that will differ radically from your normal one. You should prepare yourself to be tolerant of uncomfortable bus trips and food you cannot recognize. You might encounter people with different concepts about time and personal space. Be ready to learn about and observe differences without being judgmental. The differences you observe while abroad will undoubtedly enrich your understanding of your own culture. By stepping outside of what is familiar, you can explore what you know with a more critical, contemplative eye.

Americans abroad often have stereotypes to battle. The more you learn about local customs, beliefs, and language, both before you go and on the spot, the more people will be eager to help you learn. By showing a genuine interest and respect for local customs and culture, you show that you are not the typical "know-it-all Westerner" they may expect.

When you decide which country you will be visiting, you should learn as much as possible about all aspects of the daily life, culture, people, food, climate and terrain of your destination. Go to your local library and read travel books, historical and political studies, novels from and about your country, and relevant magazine and newspaper articles. Seek opportunities to see movies, both documentary and feature films, about the country and the region. You can also get information on various countries from travel agencies and universities, as well as from the national tourist offices of the countries you will be visiting.

Before your trip, you might also search for other Americans who have spent time in the country you'll be visiting, or citizens from there who are living in the U.S. Try contacting a nearby university to find out if foreign students would be willing to meet with you and tell you more about their homeland.

People you meet while abroad will often be very curious about life in the United States. Many people have the misconception that everyone from the United States is rich. You may want to consider bringing along some articles or booklets about problems in our country such as poverty, homelessness and environmental destruction. You might also be asked questions about U.S. foreign policies, so it's a good idea to do some research on these issues—especially on the history of U.S. policy toward the countries you will be visiting—so you can share information with others.

## Returning Home
When you return home, you will undoubtedly experience some form of culture shock. If you've been away for an extended period of time, your first trip to the supermarket may incite shock and amazement, and the experiences that make your friends complain bitterly may seem as trivial as a fly on your arm.

A productive way to deal with your feelings and heightened awareness is to get involved in some activity related to your experience overseas. Try giving talks to community, political or business groups to convey to others what you have learned. You may want to arrange interviews with local radio stations to reach a broader audience. Write articles for your local newspaper sharing your new knowledge and worldview. You might also consider getting involved in activities such as human rights work, material aid campaigns to support good grassroots projects, lobbying efforts around U.S. foreign policy issues, or nonprofit fair trade groups that import Third World crafts.

For a discussion of the various ways you can get involved, plus a list of hundreds of groups throughout the United States doing good work on Third World issues, we recommend our book *Bridging the Global Gap: A Handbook to Linking Citizens of the First and Third Worlds.* And for those particularly interested in Africa, our book *Beyond Safaris: Building People-to-People Ties with Africa* is a useful resource. To order these books and other Global Exchange resources, call us toll free at (800) 497-1994.

# 3
# WORKING IN THE
# THIRD WORLD

**M**any of the groups in this guide are small organizations with meager budgets. When sending inquiries, please enclose a large, self-addressed, stamped envelope.

For those who seek career employment with large international development agencies such as CARE, Save the Children, Church World Service and Oxfam, please refer to *Member Profiles* or *Monday Developments* put out by InterAction. (See "Guides and Publications" in Chapter 7, "Getting More Information.") InterAction is an umbrella organization of 143 international development and relief agencies.

Such groups require job seekers to have professional skills and several years of overseas experience. Some of the following groups offer a way to get started. Others look for those who already have medical, technical, or other skills.

### Agua Para La Vida (APLV)

823 Cornell Ave.
Albany, CA 94706
(510) 528-8318 or 643-8003; fax (510) 528-1519
aplv@igc.org
http://www.ced.berkeley.edu/cedr/aplv/

APLV assists rural communities in Nicaragua in attaining clean drinking water. Two to three volunteers each year live in the project community as technical advisors and teachers. Volunteers must have some experience in one of the following areas: topographical surveying, carpentry, hydraulics, plumbing, or community organizing. Self-motivation and fluency in Spanish are essential. Travel, health insurance and a stipend are provided.

### American Field Service Intercultural Programs (AFS)

198 Madison Ave., 8th floor
New York, NY 10016
(212) 299-9000, (800) 876-2376, or (800) AFS-INFO (237-4636); fax (212) 299-9090
afsinfo@afs.org
http://www.afs.org/usa

Celebrating 50 years of service in 1997, the AFS is the most experienced high-school international exchange program in the world. AFS programs help students learn to deal with diversity and understand different cultures. Programs offered in the Third World serve locations in Africa, Asia, Latin America and Eastern Europe. These include Summer and Interim Community Service and Team Mission programs in Argentina, Bolivia, Brazil, China, Colombia, Costa Rica, Ghana, Panama, Paraguay, Russia, Thailand and Venezuela. (Also see entry in Chapter 5, "Study Opportunities")

## American Friends Service Committee (AFSC)
1501 Cherry St.
Philadelphia, PA 19102-1479
(215) 241-7295
hpollock@afsc.org

In conjunction with various Mexican organizations, AFSC cosponsors summer community-service projects lasting six to eight weeks. Approximately 50 volunteers serve in small teams that work and live in villages. Applicants should be 18-24 years old, fluent in Spanish and have skills in construction, gardening, arts and crafts, child care, or other practical areas; a strong prior experience in social justice work is especially helpful. The cost is $900, which covers orientation, room and board, and health and accident insurance. A limited number of scholarships are available.

## American Refugee Committee (ARC)
2344 Nicollet Ave., Suite 350
Minneapolis, MN 55404
(612) 872-7060, fax (612) 872-4309
kraus024@maroon.tc.umn.edu
http://www.charity.org, www.interaction.org

The ARC sends medical and health personnel to provide health care and training to refugees and internally-displaced persons in Bosnia, Cambodia, Croatia, Guinea, Rwanda, Somalia, the Sudan, Thailand, Uganda and Zaire. The ARC provides a monthly stipend, group housing, health insurance, transportation and visa procurement. Length of service is usually one year. Previous overseas experience and language skills are generally required.

## Amigos de las Americas
5618 Star Ln.
Houston, TX 77057
(713) 782-5290 or (800) 231-7796; fax (713) 782-9267

info@amigoslink.org
http://www.amigoslink.org

Amigos de las Americas is a leadership-development organization that works in public health projects and fosters cross-cultural understanding throughout Latin America. Its projects are done in collaboration with the ministry of health or education of the host country. Volunteers aged 16 or older spend four to eight weeks as summer volunteers in villages in Brazil, Costa Rica, the Dominican Republic, Ecuador, Honduras, Mexico, or Paraguay. Projects include immunization, community sanitation, animal health, reforestation, teacher housing, stove construction, rabies vaccinations and dental hygiene education. Amigos chapters across the United States raise funds for the majority of volunteers and conduct their training prior to departure. If training at a chapter location is not possible, the Correspondent Volunteer Program allows youth to train through an "independent study" course. Costs range from $3000 to $3400. At least one year of high school Spanish or Portuguese is required.

## Annunciation House

1003 E. San Antonio
El Paso, TX 79901
(915) 545-4509 or 533-4675; fax (915) 544-4041

The goal of Annunciation House is to provide service and accompaniment in solidarity with the impoverished Mexican, and Central and South American communities of El Paso, TX and Juárez, Mexico. Its primary focus is in response to the needs of immigrants, refugees, the undocumented and internally displaced Mexicans living in the *colonias* of Juárez. Its ministry includes the operation of several large houses of hospitality; doing community and pastoral work in one of the *colonias* in Juárez; and operating an educational center providing border education, awareness and immersion experiences. Services offered in three houses include food, shelter, clothing and other social needs, as well as networking with immigration-asylum counselors. In addition to hospitality shelter work, placement is available for volunteers in social services, immigration/ refugee services, basic health care, border education/research, office and computer assistance, accounting and bookkeeping, building construction and maintenance, community development and work with Christian base communities. Length of volunteer service is normally one year, although shorter terms are sometimes possible. Ten-week summer internships are also available. Volunteers must be Christian, single or married without dependents, and at least 20 years old. A college education and facility with Spanish are helpful. Room and board and minor medical expenses are covered. Volunteers live at one of the houses of hospitality or in adjacent housing with one or two roommates.

## Architects and Planners in Support of Nicaragua (APSNICA)

FUNDECI Program
c/o U.S. Nicaragua Friendship Office
337 North Carolina Ave. SE
Washington, DC 20003
(202) 546-0915, fax (202) 546-0935
nicafriends@igc.apc.org

The APSNICA/FUNDECI Program provides material and technical services to various organizations and community groups in Nicaragua. Assistance is provided in a variety of areas such as accounting, agronomy, architecture, computer programming, construction, economics, engineering, forestry, health, hydrology, mechanics, nutrition, surveying, teaching, veterinary medicine and women's programs. The program accepts both skilled and unskilled volunteers who have some facility with Spanish. Volunteers pay their own expenses which vary depending on their placement. Through the U.S. Nicaragua Friendship Office, the APSNICA/FUNDECI Program also hosts delegations to Nicaragua.

## Association for International Practical Training (AIPT)

10 Corporate Center, Suite 250
10400 Little Patuxent Pkwy.
Columbia, MD 21044-3510
(410) 997-2200, fax (410) 992-3924
aipt@aipt.org
http://www.aipt.org

The AIPT is a nonprofit organization that helps to arrange on-the-job training programs abroad for students, recent graduates and young professionals in most majors and career fields. The AIPT can assist U.S. residents interested in going to over 60 selected countries in Africa, Asia, Latin America, Western and Eastern Europe and the former Soviet Union, or can help international residents arrange to train in the United States. Placement assistance is available for college students majoring in technical subjects. There is a nominal fee required to participate in the program; however, the host employer often assumes responsibility for the cost. In addition, the host employer is required to pay the trainee a salary which is competitive for the country in which he or she is working.

## Bikes Not Bombs (BNB)
59 Amory St., #103A
Roxbury, MA 02119
(617) 442-0004, fax (617) 445-2439
bnbrox@igc.apc.org

Bikes Not Bombs is a nonprofit, grassroots development and solidarity organization that helps local groups form ecologically viable bicycle workshops and related projects in Central America, Haiti and the United States. BNB provides technical assistance, training, tools and financing for these projects, as well as vocational education for inner city youth and adults in Boston. Limited field opportunities are available for experienced bilingual mechanics and personnel.

## Brethren Volunteer Services (BVS)
1451 Dundee Ave.
Elgin, IL 60120
(847) 742-5100 or (800) 323-8039; fax (847) 742-6103
cob.bvs.parti@ccunet.org

This Christian service program places volunteers in locally sponsored projects in the Middle East, Latin America, the Caribbean and Europe; and limited projects in Africa and Asia for a period of two years. They also have one-year programs in the United States. Volunteers work in community services such as education, health care and homeless shelters. Volunteers need not be Brethren but must be willing to explore the Christian faith and be willing to serve. A college degree or equivalent life experience is necessary for placement outside the U.S. Transportation to and from the project, room and board, medical coverage and a small monthly stipend are provided.

## Casa de los Amigos
Service and Education Project
Ignacio Mariscal 132
06030 Mexico, D.F.
Mexico
(52-5) 705-0521, fax (52-5) 705-0771
amigos@laneta.apc.org

Casa de los Amigos is a Quaker center of hospitality, volunteer service and cross-cultural dialogue in the heart of Latin America's largest urban megalopolis. The Service and Education Project places Spanish-speaking interns with local service organizations and community projects for full-time volunteer work of six months or more. Interns choose from among several placements, which include programs addressing issues of poverty, education, women and gender, street children, AIDS, refugees, the environment and human rights. Interns pay a placement fee of $50 plus $25 per month during the first six months of service. No specific skills are necessary and openings are regularly available. (Also see entry in Chapter 6, "Socially Responsible Travel")

## Catholic Network of Volunteer Service
4121 Harewood Rd. NE
Washington, DC 20017
(202) 529-1100 or (800) 543-5046; fax (202) 526-1094
cnvs@ari.net
http://www2.ari.net/home3/cnvs/cnvshome.html
The Catholic Network of Volunteer Service acts as a coordinating center for currently 184 Catholic and Christian organizations which need volunteers and/or lay missioners to carry out their mission in the U.S. or abroad. There are placements in over 90 countries abroad, including locations in Africa, Asia, Latin America, Eastern Europe and the former Soviet Union. Programs can be either long- or short-term and most of them provide a stipend. The Network publishes *Response,* a free annual directory of volunteer and lay-ministry opportunities.

## Centro Internacional de Solidaridad (CIS) (International Solidarity Center)
c/o Committee in Solidarity with the People of El Salvador (CISPES)
P.O. Box 1801
New York, NY 10159
(212) 229-1290, fax (212) 645-6657
cispesnatl@igc.apc.org
or
Urbanización Padilla Cuéllar
Pasaje Los Pinos, #17
San Salvador, El Salvador
(011-503) 225-0076, fax (011-503) 225-0076
cis@nicarao.apc.org
CISPES is the U.S. contact for the San Salvador-based International Solidarity Center (CIS). The CIS assists U.S., Canadian and European

organizations by organizing delegations, coordinating a human rights rapid-response network, disseminating information and facilitating "sistering" relationships between North American/European and Salvadoran cities or states. The CIS needs volunteers for these activities and also provides placement with Salvadoran organizations at the organization's request. Through the volunteer placement program, volunteers receive orientation materials, assistance in finding housing and coordination help. The CIS also coordinates an English-language school which, along with the Escuela de Español "Melida Anaya Montes", always needs volunteer teachers. (See entry in Chapter 5, "Study Opportunities")

To volunteer at the CIS in the human rights program, English teaching, or other CIS programs, individuals must make a commitment of at least three months and have sufficient money to pay for living expenses ($300-$400 per month). To be placed with a Salvadoran organization, individuals must pay a placement fee of $150, test out at an intermediate level of conversational Spanish and be interviewed in El Salvador before they can be accepted. Contact the CIS to obtain information on which organizations are currently in need of volunteers.

## CHP International
1040 North Blvd., #220
Oak Park, IL 60301
(708) 848-9650, fax (708) 848-3191

CHP International is a training contractor for several Peace Corps-country programs and regularly seeks trainers in a wide variety of technical areas for short-term (four-month) overseas assignments. In general, CHP seeks individuals with at least two years of overseas experience in a developing country. Most of their projects are in Africa or Latin America and require fluency in Spanish or French. All CHP positions require demonstrated skills as a trainer using non-formal, experiential, adult-education methods. The technical skills in which the CHP trains volunteers cover a wide range of development areas, including TEFL/ESL, primary and secondary education, math and science teaching, environmental education, agricultural extension, small business development and community development.

## Christian Peacemaker Teams (CPT)
P.O. Box 6508
Chicago, IL 60680-6508
(312) 455-1199, fax (312) 455-1199

cpt@igc.apc.org
http://www.prairienet.org/cpt/
or
c/o Christian Peacemakers Corps Office
950 Heather Dr.
Blacksburg, VA 24060
(540) 951-2788
cpt2@igc.apc.org

CPT offers an organized nonviolent alternative to war and other forms of deadly conflict between groups. CPT provides skilled support to individuals and groups committed to faith-based nonviolent action in situations where violence is an immediate reality or is supported by public policy. CPT seeks to enlist the response of the whole church in conscientious objection to war, in the development of nonviolent institutions and in skilled peacemaking ministries in situations where violent crisis threatens. Full-time Corps members are committed to a three-year term of active peacemaking service in North American and international locations. Project sites vary and include such places as Washington DC, Haiti and Hebron in the Israeli-occupied West Bank. The minimum age for participation is 21 years. Other requirements include a faith-based commitment to nonviolence, training or experience in nonviolent direct action and a willingness to live and work as part of a team focused on violence reduction. Volunteers work with local support groups in communicating CPT's vision to their home communities and in raising funds to support the cost of volunteer involvement. Full-time volunteers receive a minimal stipend toward living costs.

## Christian Service International (CSI)
804 W. McGalliard Rd.
Muncie, IN 47303-1764
(317) 286-0711, fax (317) 286-5773

CSI is an evangelical, interdenominational, nonprofit Christian service organization, promoting missions and mission projects worldwide. CSI organizes work projects, music and personal evangelical programs, vacation Bible schools, medical and dental teams and other assistance services. In addition, CSI channels materials and funds from donors to churches, schools, hospitals and other groups overseas and at home. CSI also provides missionary speakers for churches and conducts missions conferences. All CSI staff members raise their own support through financial contributions from friends, family and churches. CSI teams work throughout the United States and around various areas in Central and South America and the Caribbean, particularly in Barbados, Grenada, Guatemala, Haiti, Honduras, Jamaica and Panama. CSI has year-round volunteer programs and Team Projects in Jamaica and Haiti, as well as an Extended-Ministries Program in Jamaica. Applicants for the Extended-Ministries Program must be 19 years old or have completed at least one year of college. Individuals high-school age and older are welcome on other teams.

## Citizens Democracy Corps (CDC)

1400 I St. NW, Suite 1125
Washington, DC 20005
(202) 872-0933 or (800) 394-1945; fax (202) 872-0923

The CDC is a private, nonprofit organization that mobilizes the volunteer resources of the U.S. private sector to assist the development of market economies and democratic societies in Central and Eastern Europe and Russia. The CDC's Enterprise and Economic Development Program enlists senior-level volunteers with at least ten years' experience as entrepreneurs or corporate executives to provide on-site technical, management and marketing assistance to small- and medium-sized companies and business-support institutions in the region. Funded by private contributions and the U.S. Agency for Economic Development, the CDC's programs are located in Bulgaria, Poland, Romania, Russia and the Ukraine. Volunteer Advisors are assigned on-site for up to two months. The CDC pays round-trip international airfare. Host organizations provide housing, interpreters and local transportation. Volunteers cover personal costs such as food and other daily expenses.

## Committee for Health Rights in the Americas (CHRIA)

474 Valencia St., #120
San Francisco, CA 94110
(415) 431-7760, fax (415) 431-7768
chria@igc.apc.org

CHRIA is an organization of health-care workers and others committed to health rights across borders. CHRIA administers the Training Exchange program which places health-care professionals in medical, nursing and other health-care training institutions in El Salvador and Nicaragua. The purpose of the Training Exchange is to promote self-sufficiency by strengthening existing curricula. Volunteers provide primary health care while training future generations of health-care providers. Volunteers must be fluent in Spanish and able to make a minimum commitment of six months. Travel expenses and a minimal stipend are provided. CHRIA also works in support of immigrant and refugee health rights and has projects in El Salvador, Guatemala, Mexico and Nicaragua.

CHRIA organizes the Annual North America-Nicaragua Colloquium on Health in conjunction with the National University (UNAN), the Autonomous University of the Atlantic Coast (URACCAN) and the Nicaraguan health worker's union (FETSALUD). Delegates participate in ten days of professional/technical exchange with their Nicaraguan counterparts at various sites in Managua and on the Atlantic Coast. In-country expenses (including all fees for the Colloquium) begin at $750 and scholarships are available.

## Concern/America

P.O. Box 1790
Santa Ana, CA 92702
(714) 953-8575, fax (714) 953-1242

Concern/America is a refugee aid and development organization which places volunteers in El Salvador, Guatemala, Honduras, Mexico and Mozambique. Volunteers must have a degree in public health, nutrition, agriculture, engineering, or medicine and be at least 21 years old. Placements are for a minimum of one year. Language requirements are Spanish or (in Mozambique) Portuguese. Room, board, round-trip transportation, insurance and a monthly stipend of $50 are provided. In addition, a repatriation allowance of $50 per month of service is placed in an account in the United States.

## Conflict Resolution Catalysts (CRC)

P.O. Box 836
Montpelier, VT 05601
(802) 229-1165, fax (802) 229-1166
gshapirocrc@igc.apc.org

CRC's mission is to encourage, empower and support citizens to be active participants in peacemaking and to promote the education and use of nonviolent cooperative conflict-resolution methods and approaches. CRC coordinates the "Hope for the Future/People Connection" Project in Bosnia which seeks to facilitate long-term peace-building through conflict-resolution education, dialogue, community-building, reconciliation and the development of civil society. Core programs include community peace centers in both Sarajevo and Banja Luka; joint local/international "Neighborhood Facilitator" teams to reduce tension through mediation, human rights monitoring and local trust-building activities; youth, culture and psychological support programs; community-oriented media; and facilitation of relationships, dialogues and activities between people on all sides and with citizens in all countries.

CRC seeks volunteers to assist in these programs in Bosnia. Participants must have relevant program skills; sound physical and mental health; the ability to improvise, work in a team and adjust to difficult conditions; patience; good communication and listening skills; knowledge of the Bosnian situation; political neutrality; and cultural sensitivity. Volunteers attend a five-day training and orientation session, make a minimum three-month commitment and cover the cost of board and traveling to and from Bosnia. CRC provides housing and local travel. Stipends may be available.

## Cristianos por la Paz en El Salvador (CRISPAZ)
1135 Mission Rd.
San Antonio, TX 78210
(210) 534-6996, fax (210) 534-4995
crispaz@igc.apc.org
http://www.csn.net/cbws/rellit/

Volunteers work for a minimum of one year with responsibilities in one or more community programs. Placements are in teaching, agriculture, health care, or pastoral ministry. Volunteers must have a sponsoring community that provides a monthly stipend and all other material needs. Volunteers must speak Spanish and have skills relevant to the assignment. CRISPAZ also offers one- to two-week immersion experiences in El Salvador. These peace education encounters can be focused on religious, historical, economic, political, or ecological aspects of Salvadoran reality.

## Cross-Cultural Solutions
965 Stunt Rd.
Calabasas, CA 91302
(818) 222-8300 or (800) 380-4777; fax (818) 222-8315
ccsmailbox@aol.com
http://emol.org/emol/projectindia

Cross-Cultural Solutions' Project India offers rewarding and challenging three-week work programs year-round. Project India focuses on health, education, community development, women in development, arts and more. The program is open to people of all ages and backgrounds and no skills or experience are required. The tax-deductible program fee of $1650 covers all expenses in India such as meals, lodging and orientation/

training; airfare is not included. Extended stay programs are also available. Future programs are being planned for the Navajo reservation and West Africa. (Also see entry in Chapter 6, "Socially Responsible Travel")

## Dental Health International
847 S. Milledge Ave.
Athens, GA 30605
(706) 546-1716, fax (706) 546-1715

Dental Health International recruits dentists to work in Bhutan, Cameroon, the Cook Islands, Rwanda and Thailand for three months. A degree in dentistry is required. Volunteers pay for their own transportation. Room and board are provided.

## Dooley Foundation—Intermed
42 Lexington Ave., Suite 2428
New York, NY 10170
(212) 687-3620, fax (212) 599-6137

The Dooley Foundation recruits volunteers to work in medical projects in Asia and Central America. Projects include disease prevention, health education and research. Volunteers needed are nurses, physical therapists and medical technicians. Volunteers serve a minimum of 24 months and receive room, board, travel, health insurance and a modest stipend.

## El Porvenir
P.O. Box 1213
Ventura, CA 93001
(805) 653-1488, fax (805) 653-1255

El Porvenir offers two-week brigades to Nicaragua. Small groups (up to ten people) of North Americans join local rural families in the construction of simple potable water projects or latrines. Each work experience includes two days of interviews and activities in and around Managua at the beginning and end of the program, as well as a weekend at the beach. The group is accompanied at all times by bilingual U.S. staff. The cost of each trip is $600 (including all food, lodging and transportation in the country) plus airfare to Nicaragua. A one-week educational tour in comfortable buses and hotels is also offered in January or February.

## Esperança
1911 W. Earl Dr.
Phoenix, AZ 85015

(602) 252-7772, fax (602) 340-9197
esperanca@igc.apc.org
http://esperanca.org
   Esperança has one volunteer operation on the Amazon River in Brazil. Opportunities are available to board-certified physicians. Volunteers stay one week to six months. Room and board are provided.

## The Flying Doctors
P.O. Box 445
Los Gatos, CA 95031-0445
(800) 585-4568
http://USERS.aol.com/MTrescott/lmv/index.htm
   The Flying Doctors provide medical care to Northern Mexico and Baja California. Volunteer health professionals, translators and pilots leave for Mexico the second Thursday of every month and return on Sunday. Volunteers cover their own costs, which range from $225 to $250.

## The Flying Samaritans
P.O. Box 633
Sonora, CA 95370
(209) 532-5946 or (800) 775-9018; fax (209) 525-9018
mikeav8r@s2.sonnet.com
http://www.geocities.com/Heartland/Plains/1134
   Founded in 1961, the Flying Samaritans now maintain 24 medical clinics in Baja California. Volunteers include doctors, dentists, dental hygienists, optometrists, nurses, translators and private pilots. Volunteers, who pay their own expenses, fly to a clinic one Friday each month to provide medical care on Saturday. The projects are affiliated with the University of Tijuana and are not meant to compete with or substitute for Mexican government health programs.

## Foundation for Sustainable Development (FSD)
P.O. Box 37
Carrboro, NC 27510
(919) 932-5975, fax (919) 932-5975
arobb@email.unc.edu
   FSD is dedicated to the support of sustainable development initiatives by organizations in Latin America. It provides economic alternatives for students who want hands-on development experience in Latin America by placing them in internships with grassroots development organizations in

Guatemala and Nicaragua. FSD has summer internship programs and specialized internship programs year-round. Summer programs are eight weeks long; specialized internships vary in length. The cost of these programs vary. The cost of summer internship programs begins at $1395 and includes all room and board, in-country transportation, orientation, midterm and final evaluation, in-country and U.S. administration, as well as organizational support for the host grassroots organization. Airfare is not included. Interns must be enrolled in or past their sophomore year in college, have some ability in conversational Spanish, and be interested in development issues. FSD also provides study opportunities year-round in Guatemala.

## Fourth World Movement
7600 Willow Hill Dr.
Landover, MD 20785
(301) 336-9489, fax (301) 336-0092
4thworld@his.com

Fourth World Movement is the U.S. branch of the international organization, ATD Fourth World, which is devoted to fighting extreme poverty. Fourth World Movement's projects build on the strengths of the family and especially on the hopes parents have for their children. Two three-month internships are held in the U.S. each year as an orientation program for those considering volunteering for at least two years. These internships are designed for Americans, and the minimum age is 19. Interns and volunteers receive free housing, and a small stipend is provided for volunteers after the internship.

## Friends of the Joint Assistance Center in the Americas
P.O. Box 14481
Santa Rosa, CA 95402-6481
(707) 573-1740, fax (707) 528-8917
jacusa@aol.com

The Joint Assistance Center (JAC) is a nongovernmental voluntary group headquartered in the outskirts of New Delhi, India. The JAC offers international volunteer programs such as sanitation and building construction projects in village workcamps, working with children in schools and orphanages, and environmentally-oriented treks in the Himalayan area. The minimum commitment for most JAC programs is one month, while volunteers working with children must serve for at least three months. Room, board and administrative costs are covered by a monthly contribution of $125. Volunteers working with children should be prepared to learn some basic Hindi, preferably starting before they leave for India. Those with special skills in the areas of medicine, journalism and engineering may participate in individually designed projects that involve a long-term commitment.

## Frontier Internship in Mission
International Coordinating Office
Ecumenical Centre
P.O. Box 2100
150 route de Ferney
1211 Geneva 2
Switzerland
(41-22) 798-89-87, fax (41-22) 791-03-61
telex 23-423 OIK CH

This international ecumenical program provides people aged 20-35 with the opportunity to work abroad on social justice and theological issues. Interns throughout the world are sent from an organization in their own country to work with one based in another nation, for a period of two years. A relationship between those two organizations is developed through the intern. Travel and modest living expenses are paid by the coordinating office. The intern's overseas assignment is followed by one year of reintegration work in his or her home country.

## Genesis II
Apartado 655
7050 Cartago
Costa Rica
(011-506) 381-0739, fax (011-506) 551-0070

Genesis II seeks to preserve the Costa Rican tropical cloud forest, engaging in a broad-based program of restoration. During nine 28-day periods, up to 60 volunteers a year are employed primarily in trail construction and maintenance, tree planting and cultivation, and nursery work. Other activities include landscaping, surveying, gardening and computer work. Volunteers must be over 21 and some background or interest in environmental issues is preferred. The cost for four weeks of service is $600, which includes room, full board and laundry. (Also see entry in Chapter 6, "Socially Responsible Travel")

## Get Away Give Away (GAGA)
Eugene Friends Church
3495 W. 18th Ave.
Eugene, OR 97402
(541) 345-8054, fax (541) 345-8054
efc@efn.org

GAGA is a ministry to the people of Baja California and Sonora, Mexico. In cooperation with the Mexican government, GAGA builds homes for the homeless or for families with inadequate housing and no wage earners. This is a program for groups or teams (not individuals) from religious entities within the U.S. GAGA paves the way for projects and provides a video of potential sites and an operations manual with detailed directions about how a group can proceed to organize its missions trip. At the site, youth groups and other participants have an opportunity to participate in every aspect of building the 320-square-foot houses and in various types of building assistance to local churches. Participants share a meal and worship with the local church body and try to immerse themselves in the community while there. Care is taken to assist in a given location for only two years, so that the economy will not become dependent upon outside resources.

## Global Exchange (GX)
2017 Mission Street, #303
San Francisco, CA 94110
(415) 255-7296, fax (415) 255-7498
gx-info@globalexchange.org
http://www.globalexchange.org

Global Exchange's Reality Tours program offers work opportunities at Mar de Jade, an oceanfront retreat and language center in the Pacific coast town of Chacala (near Puerto Vallarta) in Mexico. Individuals can work in a nearby community or at the center in a number of ways, such as helping at a health clinic or teaching English in a nearby school. Volunteers live at the center for $650 per month, which includes room and board. For an additional $270 per month, Spanish study is available for 15 hours per week.

GX also coordinates four volunteer placement programs through its Mexico Program:

1) GX helps in the placement of health professionals, veterinarians and agronomists with Mexican NGOs and community-based development organizations in Chiapas.

2) GX's also coordinates internships with pro-democracy and human rights organizations in Mexico City. Volunteer interns, who must have a bachelor's degree, play a vital role in helping connect the Mexican democracy movement to international resources and support.

3) GX's International Peace Center, located in San Cristóbal de las Casas, serves as a resource for international volunteers and people interested in learning about Chiapas. The Center needs long-term volunteers to maintain the office; write and disseminate reports on local events, human rights concerns and the ongoing peace process; help coordinate peace camp volunteers, human rights delegations and visitors to the center; and provide support to Mexican human rights organizations and NGOs. Housing is provided. Volunteers participate in an initial two-day training session in San Francisco.

4) Volunteers may also work in the International Peace Center's Civilian Peace Camps, accompanying indigenous villagers living in remote camps in areas occupied by the Mexican army. The length of service is six to eight weeks.

These programs require fluency in Spanish, prior experience in Latin America or in community organizations, and good "people skills." Volunteers in the Mexico City internship, the International Peace Center or the Civilian Peace Camps need sufficient funding for a minimum stay of six months.

Global Exchange also helps place U.S. women with women's organizations in Brazil. Volunteers must be conversive in Portuguese and commit to a minimum of three months.

## Global Routes
1814 7th St., Suite A
Berkeley, CA 94710
(510) 848-4800, fax (510) 848-4801
globalrts@aol.com
http://www.lanka.net/globalrts

Global Routes interns go to remote Costa Rican, Ecuadoran Kenyan, Thai, or Navajo Nation villages where they teach math, English, science, environmental studies, or health care in a school and complete at least one community project. The internship is designed for college students 17-25 years old. Placement is offered in the summer, fall and spring. Interns live in a traditional family dwelling and participate in the daily life and ritual of their village community. This program is for people who have a passion for adventure, social contribution, cross-cultural friendship and personal growth. Tuition for the program is $3000, and college credit is available.

## Global Service Corps (GSC)
Earth Island Institute
300 Broadway, Suite 28
San Francisco, CA 94133-3312
(415) 788-3666 ext. 128; fax (415) 788-7324
gsc@igc.apc.org
http://www.earthisland.org/ei/gsc/gschome.html

GSC sends adults over 18 from all walks of life to Costa Rica, Guatemala, Kenya and Thailand, where they work with a rural community, demonstrating appropriate forms of sustainable agriculture, teaching English, building trails in the rainforest, or educating villagers on AIDS awareness issues. Participants get to know their host country from the inside out by living the day-to-day life of a small village while staying with local families. GSC seeks to show North Americans the challenges of life in developing countries while contributing something useful to the host community and their environment. Participants should be flexible and willing to learn from host communities. Sightseeing time in capital cities, two-day safaris and visits to local rainforests, lakes, or hotsprings punctuate the projects; however, participants should see this as an opportunity to do service, not just a unique vacation. Short-term projects are two to three weeks long, are available year-round and cost between $1495 and $1695. Both airfare and land costs are fully tax-deductible to the extent allowed by law. Long-term placements of two months or more are also available; however, costs vary for long-term projects. Students in GSC programs may receive internship or independent-study credit through their school, or through GSC's educational affiliate.

## Global Volunteers
375 E. Little Canada Rd.
St. Paul, MN 55117
(612) 482-1074 or (800) 487-1074; fax (612) 482-0915
email@globalvlntrs.org
http://www.globalvlntrs.org/globalvol/gvhome.htm

Global Volunteers forms teams of 8-20 volunteers who live in small communities for one to three weeks to work with local people on development projects selected by the host community. The projects may involve teaching English or business, construction and renovation of schools and clinics, health care, tutoring, business planning, or assisting in other local activities. Opportunities are available in China, Costa Rica, Ecuador, Greece, Indonesia, Italy, Jamaica, Mexico, Poland, the former Soviet

Union, Spain, Tanzania, Turkey and Vietnam. Volunteers can also serve in the Mississippi Delta, the Ozark Mountains, or the Rio Grande Valley in the United States. Volunteers come from all backgrounds and occupations, including teachers, carpenters, homemakers, physicians and artists. No special skills or languages are required. Trip costs range from $350 to $2150 and include training, visas, ground transportation, hotels, village lodging, food and project expenses. All costs are tax-deductible.

## Habitat for Humanity International

121 Habitat St.
Americus, GA 31709
(912) 924-6935 ext. 549; fax (912) 928-3655
GVWC@habitat.org
http://www.habitat.org/gv/

Habitat for Humanity places volunteers for three-year periods in Africa, Asia and the Pacific Islands, Latin America and Eastern Europe. These International Partners work in community development, primarily by helping local committees to build decent, low-cost homes in partnership with the needy, who purchase them at no interest. Volunteers must be 21 years or older. They receive a monthly stipend, housing, health insurance and travel expenses.

Habitat for Humanity also coordinates the Global Village Workcamp program in which volunteers, in teams of 10-30 people, work for one to three weeks. Costs vary according to the location of their placement. Volunteers in this program must be at least 18 and cover their own expenses.

## Health Volunteers Overseas

P.O. Box 65157, Washington Station
Washington, DC 20035-5157
(202) 296-0928, fax (202) 296-8018

Health Volunteers Overseas sends volunteers to Africa, Asia, the Caribbean and South America to improve health care through the training and education of health-care workers in their host country. Volunteers are needed in the fields of orthopedics, anesthesiology, dentistry, general surgery, oral and maxillofacial surgery, pediatrics, physical therapy and internal medicine. Volunteers usually serve for a minimum of one month and are responsible for travel expenses. In some cases, room and board are provided.

## Heifer Project International (HPI)

1015 Louisiana St.

Little Rock, AR 72202

(800) 422-1311, fax (501) 376-8906

74222.1542@compuserv.com

http://www.intellinet.com/Heifer

HPI is a nonprofit organization that alleviates hunger, poverty and environmental degradation through gifts of food-producing animals and by teaching ecologically-sound, sustainable agricultural practices to poor families around the world. The program offers volunteer opportunities at HPI's ranch and national office in Arkansas; additional opportunities are available at short-term workcamps in such places as Bolivia, the Dominican Republic, Ecuador, Honduras and Mexico. Every year, several groups travel for 8-12 days and help build facilities for HPI projects, while learning about development issues through rural village life. Volunteers should be healthy, physically fit and willing pay their own expenses, which usually range from $1000 to $1400.

## Institute for International Cooperation and Development (IICD)

1117 Hancock Rd.

P.O. Box 103

Williamstown, MA 01267

(413) 458-9828, fax (413) 458-3323

iicd1@berkshire.net

http://www.berkshire.net/~iicd1

The IICD offers solidarity work programs to Angola, Brazil, Mozambique, Nicaragua and Zimbabwe. The projects abroad include teaching in schools for street children, vocational schools and teacher training colleges; educating rural families about health and nutrition; assisting in preschool activities; constructing schools and latrines; and planting trees. Volunteers also travel to Southern Africa and collect information for use in U.S. classrooms. Volunteers undergo preparatory language and practical training at the IICD before going overseas. Projects last 5-20 months and are offered throughout the year. To start in a program, volunteers must be 18 years of age. The tuition fees range from $3400 to $4600. It includes food and lodging, airfare and stay abroad, international insurance and vaccinations.

## Institute of Cultural Affairs (ICA)

4220 N. 25th St.

Phoenix, AZ 85016

(602) 955-4811 or (800) 742-4032; fax (602) 954-0563

icaphoenix@igc.apc.org

Independent national Institutes operate in 26 countries in North America, Africa, Asia, Latin America and Europe. Limited opportunities exist for volunteers in community-based development programs, preferably for a two-year period. City offices need people with computer and facilitation skills. Domestic apprenticeships are available for work with educational ventures, multicultural populations and neighborhoods of the Southwest United States. Volunteers must pay transportation and living expenses, the latter ranging from $125 to $350 per month. Apprentices can receive small stipends.

## International Association for Exchange of Students for Technical Experience (IAESTE)

c/o Association for International Practical Training (AIPT)

10400 Little Patuxent Pkwy., Suite 250

Columbia, MD 21044-3510

(410) 997-3068, fax (410) 997-5186

iaeste@aipt.org

http://www.aipt.org

IAESTE arranges reciprocal exchanges between over 60 member countries for college students in engineering, architecture, mathematics, computer science, agriculture and the sciences to obtain on-the-job practical training with host employers in other countries. The member countries are located in all of the following regions: Africa, Asia, Latin America, Eastern and Western Europe and the former Soviet Union. The IAESTE program is administered in the U.S. by the Association for International Practical Training (AIPT). (See entry in this chapter.)

## International Fellows Program

International Foundation for Education and Self Help (IFESH)

5040 E. Shea Blvd.

Phoenix, AZ 85254

(602) 443-1800

The International Fellows Program places U.S. graduate students and college seniors in projects in sub-Saharan Africa. Fellows assist in community-based endeavors, which may include teaching, or the development of small-business enterprises, health initiatives, or skills-training programs. Students with backgrounds in areas such as agriculture, health administration, computer science, medicine, veterinary medicine, the sciences, business administration, literacy and education are particularly encouraged to apply. Applicants should be prepared to live in a Third World environment. Good communication and writing skills are necessary; fluency in a foreign language, particularly French, is desirable. In recruiting, priority is given to African-Americans, although others are welcome to apply. Fellows receive a living allowance, health insurance, round-trip travel and a monthly stipend of $800 for the nine-month program.

## International Lifeline (IL)

Box 32714
Oklahoma City, OK 73123-0914
(405) 728-2828, fax (405) 946-5512

IL is a Christian organization addressing the medical problems of the indigent in Haiti. IL places medical volunteers for primary health care or pediatric care. Patients are not charged for any medicines dispensed, but must pay a small doctor's fee. Volunteers normally serve for 10-14 days in both urban and rural locations. They must pay for all travel and related expenses. However, the total cost is usually less than $2500—while this includes airfare from Miami, it does not include hotel, meals and the purchase of medicines locally.

## International Medical Corps (IMC)

12233 W. Olympic Blvd., Suite 280
Los Angeles, CA 90064-1052
(310) 826-7800, fax (310) 442-6622
imc@igc.apc.org

IMC is a private, nonsectarian, nonpolitical, nonprofit organization established by U.S. physicians and nurses in 1984 to provide health care and training to devastated areas worldwide. Current projects are located in Afghanistan, Angola, Bosnia-Herzegovina, Burundi, Rwanda, Somalia and the Sudan. IMC seeks individuals with medical expertise, especially orthopedic and general surgeons, pediatricians, registered nurses, public-health workers and community-health worker trainers. IMC offers paid and volunteer positions. Room and board are provided. Other forms of compensation include round-trip transportation, medical insurance and a small salary.

## International Rescue Committee (IRC)
122 E. 42nd St.
New York, NY 10168-1289
(212) 551-3000, fax (212) 551-3180

The IRC was founded in 1933 at the request of Albert Einstein to help rescue victims from persecution in Nazi Germany. IRC provides direct assistance to refugees uprooted by racial, ethnic and religious violence, as well as people displaced by war, drought and famine. Projects are located in about 25 countries including Azerbaijan, Bosnia-Herzegovina, Cambodia, Georgia, Guinea, Ivory Coast, Kenya, Mozambique, Pakistan, Russia, Rwanda, Serbia, the Sudan, Tajikistan, Tanzania and Thailand. IRC recruits specialists in public health, water and sanitation and logistics for its field operations. Previous work experience in a refugee camp is preferred.

## International Schools Services (ISS)
## Educational Staffing Program
15 Roszel Rd.
P.O. Box 5910
Princeton, NJ 08543
(609) 452-0990, fax (609) 452-2690
iss@iss.edu
http://www.iss.edu

ISS provides teacher placement services for over 200 American and international schools in Africa, Asia, the Middle East, Latin America and Europe. ISS also publishes *The ISS Directory of Overseas Schools.*

## International Voluntary Workcamps (in Turkey)
## (Ulaslararasi Gönüllü Gençlik Çalisma Kamplari)
c/o Volunteers for Peace (VFP)
43 Tiffany Rd., Belmont, VT 05730-0202
(802) 259-2759
or
Gençtur
Istiklal Cad.Zambak Sok.15/5, 80080 Taksim Istanbul, Turkey
(90-212) 249-25-15, fax (90-212) 249-25-54 or 519-08-64

Gençtur's International Voluntary Workcamps offer volunteers a chance to experience the traditions of daily life in a Turkish rural village, while serving in various projects involving manual labor. Workcamps consist of international groups of 12-20 volunteers from at least four countries.

Although every group will have a bilingual leader fluent in Turkish, the common language is typically English. Volunteers are requested to respect the group leader's experience, as well as local customs; therefore an open mind, tolerance and willingness to help each other within the group are essential. Volunteers must be 18-35 years old; however, there are additional junior and teenage workcamps (for ages 9-14 and 14-18). Simple accommodations (usually in a primary school or village center) and meals are provided by the village. Fees include registration (DM100) and in-country transportation (DM10 to DM55); airfare is not included. For an additional fee of DM100, volunteers may spend the three days prior to their orientation on a sightseeing tour of Istanbul and its environs.

## International Volunteer Projects
Council on International Educational Exchange (CIEE)
205 E. 42nd St.
New York, NY 10017-5706
(212) 822-2695, fax (212) 822-2689
ivpbrochure@ciee.org
http://www.ciee.org/
    The Council's international volunteer projects are designed to promote international cooperation and understanding; among its many activities is the placement of American volunteers in workcamps abroad. Projects are located in over 30 countries in Africa, Asia, Europe and North America. In addition, a few projects are offered in Central and South America every year. Volunteers work in groups of 10-15 people for two to four weeks on local community development projects such the restoration of historic sites, renovation of community centers, or construction of affordable housing. Volunteers must be at least 18 years old and upper age limits apply in Belgium, Spain, Tunisia and Turkey due to the requirements imposed by local Youth Ministries. For projects in North Africa, conversational ability in French is required, as is Spanish for projects in Spain. Volunteers pay for their own transportation, insurance and an administrative fee of $195. Room and board are provided. (Also see entry in Chapter 5, "Study Opportunities" and Chapter 7, "Getting More Information")

## Interns for Peace (IFP)
475 Riverside Dr., 16th floor
New York, NY 10115
(212) 870-2226, fax (212) 870-2119
or

Rehove Geula 35, Tel Aviv 63304, Israel
(972-3) 517-6525 or 510-5064; fax (972-3) 517-7995

IFP is an independent, nonpolitical, community-sponsored program dedicated to building trust and respect among Jewish and Arab citizens of Israel. Interns carry out the program under staff guidance while receiving work experience in human relations, conflict resolution and group facilitation. Interns work on projects in education, sports, health, the arts, community and workplace relations and adult interest groups. A two-year commitment is required. Interns must be of Jewish or Arab descent. Other requirements include a knowledge of and commitment to furthering Jewish-Arab relations; a bachelor's degree or equivalent; proficiency in Hebrew or Arabic; a previous stay in Israel of at least six months; previous experience in community or human relations work; and a background in teaching, sports, health care, art, music, business, youth work, or community organizing. Interns are placed in communities in Israel and receive housing, a monthly stipend and health insurance.

## Interplast
300B Pioneer Wy.
Mountain View, CA 94041
(415) 962-0123, fax (415) 962-1619
interplast@worldaccess.com

Interplast is an organization of volunteer plastic surgeons, pediatricians, anesthesiologists and nurses who provide free reconstructive surgery to poor people in the Third World—people who ordinarily have no help for burns or cleft lips and palates. Interplast works in Bangladesh, Burma, Chile, the Dominican Republic, Ecuador, Honduras, Mongolia, Peru, the Philippines, Thailand and Vietnam. Placements are for two weeks. Doctors in private practice are encouraged to pay their own transportation; otherwise, transportation and housing are covered.

## Involvement Volunteers Association (IVI)
P.O. Box 218
Port Melbourne, Victoria 3207
Australia
(61-3) 9646-9392, fax (61-3) 9646-5504
ivimel@iaccess.com.au
http://www.iaccess.com.au/ivimel/home.html

Established in 1988 as a nonprofit organization, IVI provides low-cost, volunteer opportunities in as many countries as possible. Individual volunteer and group placements are available in such fields as conservation and the environment, teaching and social services. Group placements for four to ten volunteers run for two weeks, individual placements for two to twelve weeks. Placements are available in Australia, Estonia, Fiji, Finland, Germany, Ghana, India, Italy, Kenya, Lebanon, Malaysia, New Zealand, Papua New Guinea, South Africa, Thailand and (in the United States) California. The placement fee for two-week programs range from $40 to $200 (for individuals) and $120 to $200 (for groups). Programs may be extended up to 12 months, during which volunteers can accept as many placements and as many countries as they desire. Costs include an application fee of $125 and a fee of $250 for a 12-month program. The fees cover room and board. International and domestic travel, and health and accident insurance are not included.

### Jesuit Volunteers International (JVI)
P.O. Box 254878
Washington, DC 20007
(202) 687-1132, fax (202) 687-5082
JVI@gunet.georgetown.edu

JVI is a Christian program that works alongside Jesuits and local church leaders to serve the poor and disadvantaged in Belize, Chile, Jamaica, Micronesia, Nepal, Peru and Tanzania. The JVI philosophy integrates simple living in a community while working for justice and reflecting on faith. Volunteers (21 years or older) must commit to two years of service in areas such as teaching, youth ministry and social outreach. JVI provides pre-orientation and orientation programs, room and board, medical insurance, a monthly stipend and final re-orientation.

### MADRE
121 W. 27th St., Room 301
New York, NY 10001
(212) 627-0444, fax (212) 675-3704
madre@igc.apc.org

MADRE places professional women trained in midwifery, obstetrics, pediatrics, social work and stress counseling in El Salvador, Guatemala, Haiti and Nicaragua. Placements range from one to two weeks. Spanish or French fluency is preferred. Volunteers must pay for all expenses.

### Maryknoll Mission Association of the Faithful
Bethany Building

P.O. Box 307
Maryknoll, NY 10545
(914) 762-6364, fax (914) 762-7031

Maryknoll lay missioners serve for three and a half years in Africa, Asia, or Latin America. All new missioners attend a four-month Orientation to Mission program at Maryknoll, NY prior to leaving for their overseas assignment. Language training is available in the country of assignment. Volunteer opportunities include community organization, health promotion, teaching, adult education, human rights and pastoral team ministry. Applicants must be Roman Catholic; they also must have a college degree or a requisite skill, plus a minimum experience of one year after the completion of formal training. Room and board, health insurance, travel expenses and a stipend are paid by Maryknoll.

### Médécins Sans Frontières (MSF) (Doctors Without Borders)
11 E. 26th St., Suite 1906
New York, NY 10010
(212) 679-6800, fax (212) 670-7016

MSF recruits physicians (i.e., general practitioners, surgeons, obstetrician/gynecologists, pediatricians, anesthesiologists and specialists in tropical medicine or public health), nurses and nurse practitioners. The average length of service is six months; for specialists, however, service may be four to six weeks on rare occasions. Volunteers receive a stipend of approximately $700 per month in addition to airfare and housing.

### Mennonite Central Committee (MCC)
21 S. 12th St.
Akron, PA 17501-0500
(717) 859-1151, fax (717) 859-2171
mailbox@mcc.org

The MCC is the development and relief agency of Mennonite and Brethren in Christ churches in North America. MCC is committed to serving people suffering from poverty, conflict, oppression and natural disaster. In addition, MCC strives for a free interchange between the churches and community groups they serve abroad and the North American churches that support their programs. Currently 950 volunteers serve in agriculture, health, education, social services and community development in 50 countries, including locations in Africa, Asia, Latin America, Eastern Europe, the former Soviet Union and North America. Qualifications depend on each assignment. MCC asks that volunteers be Christian, actively involved in a congregation and agree to its nonviolent principles. Placements are for three years overseas, two to three years in North America. Transportation, living expenses and a small stipend are provided.

## Michigan Faith and Resistance Peace Team (MPT)

1516 Jerome St.

Lansing, MI 48912

(517) 484-3178

michpeaceteam@igc.apc.org

The MPT, spiritually-grounded in nonviolence, empowers people to engage in active nonviolent peacemaking. The MPT was founded in 1993 in response to the growing need for civilian peacemakers both internationally and within the U.S. It offers nonviolence-training workshops for local and international violence-reduction efforts, fields violence-reduction peace teams in conflict areas in the U.S. and abroad, and maintains a national pool of volunteers for these peace teams.

The MPT is currently organizing small groups of peacemakers to join the Civil Peace Camps (Campamentos Civiles por la Paz) coordinated by the Center for Human Rights in San Cristóbal de las Casas, in Chiapas, Mexico, where low-intensity warfare continues between the Mexican military and local guerrilla forces. Requirements for participants include knowledge of Spanish, some experience in dealing with conflict situations and a commitment to nonviolence. The period of service lasts about two weeks, beginning with orientation in the U.S. one day before leaving for Mexico. The total cost, including airfare, is $800 to $900. (Also see entry in Chapter 7, "Getting More Information")

## Mission Service Recruitment, Presbyterian Church USA

100 Witherspoon St., Room 3417

Louisville, KY 40202-1396

(800) 779-6779, fax (502) 569-5975

The Mission Volunteers International and Mission Volunteers USA programs give participants an opportunity to serve a variety of communities in Africa, Asia, Latin America, Western and Eastern Europe and the United States. Service opportunities are available in such areas as agriculture, education, public health, youth work, community service, community development, English as a Second Language, office administration and work at camps and conference centers. Volunteers must be active members of a Christian church community, willing to live simply, and committed to working in a community of need. A second language is desirable and may be required for some placements. Room and board are often provided. Volunteers may need to raise funds for living expenses. Length of service ranges from six months to two years.

## Nicaragua Center for Community Action (NICCA)
2140 Shattuck Ave.
Box 2063
Berkeley, CA 94704
(510) 832-4959, fax (510) 654-8635
nicca@igc.apc.org
NICCA sends work brigades of 10-20 people to Nicaragua for three weeks. Projects involve construction, reforestation, or sustainable agriculture. The groups work side by side with Nicaraguans, rebuilding their economy while continuing to support their revolution. *Brigadistas* live with families in a cooperative and experience firsthand the Nicaraguans' struggles against neo-liberal policy. The cost is $550, which includes group expenses in Nicaragua but not airfare.

## Nuestros Pequeños Hermanos
Apartado Postal 30-500
06740 Mexico 4, D.F.
Mexico
(52-5) 7313-4504, 7313-1177, or 7313-7764
fax (52-5) 7317-4477 or 7311-2655
nphintjj@mpsnet.com.mx
Volunteers serve in Father Wasson's orphanages in Haiti, Honduras, Mexico and Nicaragua, working in construction, as dorm directors in dormitories, in food preparation and as office support staff. Placements are for one year. Volunteers pay travel expenses; room and board are provided.

## Operation Crossroads Africa
475 Riverside Dr., Suite 1368
New York, NY 10115-0050
(212) 870-2106, fax (212) 870-2055
oca@igc.apc.org
Operation Crossroads Africa sends teams of 10-15 Americans to work in Africa and the Caribbean on a variety of development projects. Teams go for a period of six to eight weeks. Overseas volunteers must demonstrate an ability to work well with other cultures and races. Volunteers must raise funds for their travel; however, some scholarships are available.

## Options

Project Concern International
3550 Afton Rd.
San Diego, CA 92123
(619) 279-9690, fax (619) 694-0294
patty@projcon.cts.com
http://www.serve.com/PCI

Options is the international health-care professional recruitment and referral service of Project Concern International. Options provides volunteer opportunities linking health specialists with medical programs and missions, hospitals and clinics worldwide. Hundreds of volunteers are placed each year, including primary-care physicians, surgeons, nurses, physician assistants, public health specialists, hospital administrators and therapists. Length of service ranges from two weeks to two years. Most facilities provide room and board, and some positions pay airfare and a stipend. A newsletter, published and distributed bimonthly, lists all current volunteer opportunities. A membership fee—$25 for U.S. residents, $40 for international residents—includes a subscription to the newsletter and referral costs.

## Overseas Development Network (ODN)

333 Valencia St., Suite 330
San Francisco, CA 94103
(415) 431-4204, fax (415) 431-5953
odn@igc.org
http://www.igc.apc.org/odn/

ODN is a national network of university-based student groups working to promote long-term solutions to poverty through education and direct aid. Although ODN does not generally place volunteers directly, it does offer two summer internship opportunities, *Vamonos Rodando* and *Campamentos Juveniles,* in different parts of Mexico every year. Internship opportunities are also available in Zimbabwe to work with ODN's partner organization, Zimbabwe Friends of the Unemployed. Proficiency in the language of the country is required for placement. Interns work with community organizations, supporting local initiatives for economically sustainable development. They then return to their schools in the U.S. to help educate others on Third World problems and solutions. ODN also publishes resource guides on international development and job opportunities. ODN also publishes resource guides on international development and job opportunities and has recently established the Development Opportunities Clearinghouse, a resource and referral service for individuals interested in voluntary service through grassroots organizations overseas. Each year, the Clearinghouse handles hundreds of requests from college students, recent graduates and professionals. Most of the internships and volunteer opportunities it advertises are unpaid. Interested individuals must have some experience living overseas. (See Chapter 7, "Getting More Information")

## Pastors for Peace

610 W. 28th St.

Minneapolis, MN 55408

(612) 870-7121, fax (612) 870-7109

p4p@igc.apc.org

Pastors for Peace organizes national humanitarian aid caravans, human rights delegations, work brigades and study trips to Mexico, Central America and Cuba. Programs are designed to raise awareness throughout the U.S. about the impact of U.S. foreign policy on developing nations in this hemisphere, and to provide opportunities for the establishment of "people-to-people" relationships across borders. Pastors for Peace projects range from one week to one month and opportunities for long-term volunteer placements in human rights are available in Chiapas, Mexico. Volunteers must be fluent in Spanish and are expected to cover their own living costs. Work brigades in construction and agriculture are also offered in Mexico, Nicaragua and Cuba.

Participants are needed for the humanitarian-aid caravans to Guatemala, Mexico, Nicaragua and Cuba. Duties include driving and maintaining trucks, buses, or vans along 9-12 routes which converge in San Antonio before proceeding south. After the destination country is reached and the supplies are unloaded, volunteers can participate in a week-long educational program. (Also see entry in Chapter 6, "Socially Responsible Travel")

## Peace Brigades International (PBI)

2642 College Ave.

Berkeley, CA 94704

(510) 540-0749, fax (510) 849-1247

pbiusa@igc.apc.org

http://www.igc.apc.org/pbi/index.html

When invited, PBI sends unarmed nonpartisan international peace teams into areas of conflict and repression. Volunteers provide protective accompaniment for those whose lives have been threatened because of their own work in human rights and social change. PBI currently coordinates several projects worldwide. Volunteers for its Central America or Colombia Projects should be fluent in Spanish. PBI's other projects also have language requirements: English for Sri Lanka; French for Haiti (in addition, volunteers are expected to learn Creole after their arrival); and English or French for North America. PBI also has a project in the Balkans, in cooperation with the Balkans Peace Team International—however, English is suitable for this project. For all projects, volunteers must be 25 years or older and must participate in a PBI volunteer-training session. Volunteers usually must make a commitment of at least six months. For most PBI projects, volunteers pay transportation and health insurance; other costs are covered by PBI. Volunteers also receive a small stipend (about $50 a month) and a relocation allowance.

## Peace Corps
1990 K St. NW
Washington, DC 20526
(800) 424-8580

The Peace Corps is a U.S. government agency that sends volunteers to 95 developing countries requesting assistance. Countries involved are in Africa, Asia, Latin America, Eastern Europe and the former Soviet Union. Volunteers work in a wide range of areas, including education, public health and nutrition. The Peace Corps also has a strong environmental program. Volunteers must make a two-year commitment and have a college degree or three to five years' experience in their area of expertise. They receive training in language and cultural issues for 8-12 weeks prior to their overseas placement. The Peace Corps provides room and board and a monthly stipend. When their service is over, volunteers receive a "readjustment allowance" of $200 for every month served.

## Peacework
305 Washington St. SW
Blacksburg, VA 24060-4745
(540) 953-1376, fax (540) 552-0119
75352.261@compuserve.com

Peacework is a nonprofit organization that sponsors international service projects in developing countries. Volunteers live together and work on indigenous development projects initiated, planned and supervised by local community leaders. Projects include building houses, schools or clinics; working with children; addressing environmental issues; or providing aid in agriculture or health care. Programs include opportunities for travel, interaction with the local community, cultural events and discussions about the host country's political, social and economic influences. Volunteers may be any age or background. Projects typically last 2-3 weeks and take place during winter break, spring break and the summer. Projects may occur in such locations as Costa Rica, Cuba, the Dominican Republic, El Salvador, Ghana, Guatemala, Honduras, Mexico, Nicaragua, Russia, Vietnam or in developing communities in the United States.

Peacework also offers volunteer programs for groups of 5-50 people from colleges and universities, service organizations within churches and civic groups, and nonprofit associations. Peacework provides coordination between the volunteer group and its host organization; orientation materials addressing health and travel issues; on-site planning; insurance; interpreters; travel arrangements; and assistance with visas if needed.

## People to People International
501 E. Armour Blvd.
Kansas City, MO 64109-2200
(816) 531-4701, fax (816) 561-7502
ptpi@cctr.umkc.edu
http://cei.haag.umkc.edu/ptp

People to People International, in affiliation with the University of Missouri, Kansas City and People to People chapters worldwide, coordinates the Overseas Internship Program which provides volunteer opportunities for students. Internships are full-time positions lasting for two months and are selected in accordance with a student's academic background and career goals. Students in the program may earn three to six hours of undergraduate or graduate credit. Internships may be arranged at any time during the calendar year and may be located in Argentina, Australia, the Czech Republic, Denmark, England, Germany, Ireland, Kenya, Russia or Spain. The program fee is $1675, which includes tuition and all placement costs. Airfare and housing must be arranged separately.

## Plenty International
P.O. Box 394
Summertown, TN 38483
(615) 964-4864, fax (615) 964-4864
plenty1@usit.net
http://www.public.usit.net/plenty1/index.html

Plenty International sends a limited number of volunteers to work on community-based development projects in food production, primary health care, construction, communications and other appropriate technologies aimed at increasing local self-sufficiency in Africa, Central America, the Caribbean and Native American reservations in the U.S. The length of service varies with each position, but typically lasts one to six months. In most cases volunteers must pay all travel and living expenses. *The Plenty Bulletin,* a quarterly publication, describes all current projects and is available by mail or on the web site.

## Ponape Agriculture and Trade School (PATS)
P.O. Box 39
Pohnpei, FM 96941
(691) 320-2991, fax (691) 320-6046
info@pats.edu
http://pats.edu
PATS was founded in 1965 to prepare students in vocational skills needed throughout Micronesia, and to help them grow in their Christian faith to become responsible leaders in their communities. Its teaching staff of about 25 include Micronesians and expatriate volunteers, usually recent college graduates or people with skilled technical experience. Staff members are generally asked to spend mornings teaching in the classroom, and afternoons supervising vocational work in agriculture, construction, or mechanics. The teaching staff is predominantly Roman Catholic, though many Protestants have taught at PATS. Volunteers should teach for at least two years—however, some stay much longer. PATS provides volunteers with room and board and a small monthly stipend.

## Project HOPE
Health Sciences Education Center
Carter Hall
Millwood, VA 22646
(540) 837-2100 or (800) 544-4673; fax (540) 837-1813
cmarino@projhope.org
Project HOPE is an international nonprofit health-care education organization. The primary goal of Project HOPE is the improvement of health conditions through worldwide education. It provides specialty training in the areas of medicine, dentistry, nursing and allied health to local professionals in their own environment. Projects are located in China, Colombia, Costa Rica, the Czech Republic, Ecuador, Egypt, Guatemala, Honduras, Hungary, Kazakhstan, Macedonia, Malawi, Nicaragua, Peru,

Poland, Russia, Slovakia and Taiwan. The basic requirement for employment in Project HOPE's international programs is licensure, or in some cases certification, within a health-care occupation. Most of Project HOPE's international faculty have at least a Master's degree and academic and/or clinical teaching experience.

## Public Health International (PHI)

P.O. Box 116
Roseburg, OR 97470
(541) 672-0615
phi@wanweb.net

PHI recruits, trains and places public-health professionals with existing international relief agencies as well as within its own projects. Most volunteers work in disaster and refugee relief settings. PHI makes arrangements for travel, living expenses and stipends. Length of service ranges from a few weeks to a year.

## Quaker Overseas Volunteer Ministry

World Ministries
Friends United Meeting
101 Quaker Hill Dr.
Richmond, IN 47374
(317) 962-7573, fax (317) 966-1293
curtisb@freemark.com or firstum@earlham.edu

The Quaker Overseas Volunteer Ministry offers opportunities for ministering to persons overseas in their spiritual and/or physical needs. The Ministry operates in Africa, the Middle East, Belize, Cuba and Jamaica. A variety of volunteer assignments is available. They depend upon adequate funding for support and ministry expenses. Volunteers are provided with an adequate stipend. Occasionally, paid missionary or field staff positions are available.

## Queen Louise Home for Children

Lutheran Social Services of the Virgin Islands
P.O. Box 866
Frederiksted
St. Croix, VI 00841-0866
(809) 772-0090, fax (809) 772-0589

The Lutheran Social Services of the Virgin Islands operates residential care facilities on St. Croix and St. Thomas for children, teens, adults, seniors and the handicapped. They are a host organization of AmeriCorps, a program of the Corporation for National Service (CNS), which allows persons to serve in their communities while earning money towards college tuition or student loans.

At Lutheran Social Services' Queen Louise Home for Children, AmeriCorps members may volunteer as Cottage Parents, living with and caring for abused and neglected children aged 4-13. Volunteers must commit to a full year of service and be at least 22 years old, preferably with two years of college education. Single members must have no dependents; married couples will be considered, provided that they have no plans of getting pregnant while in service. Accommodations, utilities and basic food expenses are included. CNS provides a living stipend of $7945 per year and an education award of approximately $5000, upon completion of one year's service.

### Ramallah Friends School
P.O. Box 66
Ramallah, West Bank
Palestine (via Israel)
(972-2) 9562-0230
or
c/o World Ministries
Friends United Meeting
101 Quaker Hill Dr.
Richmond, IN 47374
(317) 962-7573, fax (317) 966-1293
firstum@earlham.edu

The Ramallah Friends School is a 103-year old primary and secondary school (grades K-12), founded by U.S. Quakers. This school educates Palestinian children in both English and Arabic, with a curriculum based on both local and U.S. educational methodologies, as well as Quaker values of nonviolence, peace, tolerance and universal humanism. Teachers are recruited from the U.S. and elsewhere, generally for a position lasting one year. Salary is commensurate with local standards and teaching qualifications. Due to the ongoing conflict in the area, applicants must be willing to endure some hardships.

### Ramallah Workcamp
World Ministries

Friends United Meeting
101 Quaker Hill Dr.
Richmond, IN 47374
(317) 962-7573, fax (317) 966-1293

The Ramallah Workcamp, located in the Palestinian West Bank, offers volunteer opportunities for two to three weeks, usually during the summer. Activities may include construction, painting and other rehabilitation projects. The program includes some studying and traveling. Participants should be 17-25 years old and do not need any special skills except an ability to listen and follow directions. Cost is estimated at $1700.

## Service Civil International-International Voluntary Service (SCI-IVS)
5474 Walnut Level Rd.
Crozet, VA 22932
(804) 823-1826, fax (804) 823-5027
sciivsusa@igc.apc.org
http://wworks.com/~sciivs/

SCI-IVS provides workcamp opportunities in Europe, Eastern Europe and North America. Limited exchange possibilities are offered in sub-Saharan Africa, South Asia and Latin America for very experienced, well-prepared and motivated volunteers. Typical camps have 8-15 volunteers and last two to three weeks; most workcamps take place between June and October. Projects range from physical labor—as in farm work, construction and renovation, or environmental cleanups—to social work—as in assisting refugees, children, the elderly, or the handicapped. Some projects, especially in Europe, offer study programs focused on a particular type of work. The minimum age for overseas camps is 18, 16 for U.S. and Canadian workcamps. Application fees are $100 for Western European camps, $50 for North American workcamps and $150 to $250 for other locations. A few special camps charge an additional fee. Volunteers must pay for their own transportation to the camp. Room and board is provided by the camp hosts. Camp listings for the summer are available in late March.

## Servicio Internacional para la Paz (SIPAZ) (International Service for Peace)
P.O. Box 2415
Santa Cruz, CA 95063
(408) 425-1257, fax (408) 425-1257
forlatam@igc.apc.org

http://www.nonviolence.org/~nvweb/sipaz

SIPAZ is a coalition of North American, Latin American and European organizations dedicated to supporting the peace process in Chiapas, Mexico. It offers long-term placements for volunteers. Duties may include maintaining links with local organizations, developing contacts with various people affected by the conflict, monitoring the peace process (including formal talks and independent initiatives), and assisting in the preparation of updates for international distribution. Volunteers should be fluent in Spanish and have prior international work experience, preferably in nonviolent peacemaking or conflict resolution. A commitment of one year or more is desirable.

### Sierra Madre Alliance

P.O. Box 41416

Tucson, AZ 85717

(520) 326-2511, fax (520) 326-2511

sierrarg@igc.apc.org

The Sierra Madre Alliance provides grassroots support and technical assistance to the indigenous communities of the Sierra Madre in Chihuahua, Mexico and assists the work of the Advisory Council of the Sierra Madre. Current projects are in construction, land restoration, sustainable agriculture and human rights. There are plans to start an ecotourism project in 1997. There are opportunities in permaculture, gardening, botany, wildlife conservation, bookbinding, business development, range management and fundraising. Volunteers must be able to speak Spanish, self-sufficient and respectful of the Tarahumara and Tepehuan native cultures. No stipends are currently available; for skilled volunteers, however, some compensation for travel and living expenses may be possible. For skilled volunteers raising their own funds, assistance also may be available.

### Sisters of Charity of the Incarnate Word

4503 Broadway

San Antonio, TX 78209

(210) 828-2224, fax (210) 828-9741

vimoffice@aol.com

Volunteers must commit themselves to working with the poor and following a simple lifestyle. The Sisters of Charity's overseas program is located in Mexico, where volunteers serve for two to three years. Volunteers must be over 21 and single or married without dependents. All types of skills are needed and prior knowledge of Spanish is required. Room and board are provided, as well as with airfare, a small monthly stipend and health insurance.

## SMA Lay Missionaries
Society of African Missions
256 N. Manor Cr.
Takoma Park, MD 20912-4561
(301) 891-2037, fax (301) 270-6370
smausa-v@ix.netcom.com

The Society of African Missions provides volunteer opportunities for lay missionaries in health, education, community development, social services, pastoral ministries, agriculture and construction. 16 lay missionaries currently serve in Ghana, the Ivory Coast, Liberia and other African countries, as well as in African-American parishes in the United States. Volunteers must be Catholic, single or married without dependents, 23-50 years old, and willing to serve for at least two years. They must also be college graduates (B.A. or B.S.), or have a similar level of qualification in their field of expertise; any previous volunteer experience is helpful. The application deadline is April 15.

An orientation program, held from September to April, emphasizes spiritual development, team building, mission theology, and ways to work in a cross-cultural setting. SMA covers room and board, medical expenses, post-orientation medical insurance, a stipend and transportation to and from the mission site. Upon their return, lay missionaries take part in a re-entry program.

## Teachers for Africa Program (TFA)
International Foundation for Education and Self-Help (IFESH)
5040 E. Shea Blvd., Suite 260
Phoenix, AZ 85254-4610
(602) 443-1800, fax (602) 443-1824

IFESH is a nonprofit development organization dedicated to improving living conditions of the poor and disadvantaged in the Third World, particularly in sub-Saharan Africa, by supporting health centers and projects in vocational training, literacy and agriculture. IFESH's Teachers for Africa Program is designed to allow teachers, university professors, school administrators and other professionals the opportunity to spend one academic year working within the educational systems of various African countries. Experienced teachers are needed in such fields as biology, chemistry, physics, mathematics, statistics, engineering, computer science, psychology, curriculum development, education, medicine, agriculture, economics, English and business administration.

Volunteers must have at least a college degree; at least three years experience as a teacher, professor or administrator; and evidence of good health. Applicants must be proficient in French in order to work in a French-speaking country. Accepted applicants must participate in a one-week orientation held in July or August in Phoenix; volunteers are also provided with in-country orientation. IFESH covers costs for placement, orientation, round-trip transportation, comprehensive insurance and a monthly stipend of up to $1000. After returning, participants are expected to help raise local understanding of issues affecting Africa by offering seminars and lectures in schools, churches and other community centers, as well as preparing articles for the local press and other publications.

## TECNICA
775 E. 19th St.
Brooklyn, NY 11230
(718) 859-4546
albondiga@igc.apc.org

TECNICA sends a limited number of volunteers to Nicaragua according to the specific needs of unions and other mass organizations. TECNICA seeks female gynecologists and health administrators for a union-run women's health clinic, and female lawyers for a women's legal clinic. Occupational health and safety volunteers are also needed. For work brigades lasting two to three weeks, TECNICA seeks volunteers in skilled trade areas such as electricians, plumbers and construction workers. Generally, all volunteers must speak Spanish, although this is not mandatory for the work brigades. No stipends are available.

## Unidas Para Vivir Mejor (UPAVIM)
5051 Eliots Oak Rd.
Columbia, MD 21044
(502) 279-9061
upavim@ns.guate.net

UPAVIM is a grassroots women's cooperative aimed at improving the women's lives in the community of La Esperanza, near Guatemala City. Applicants should be experienced tutors or teachers (especially in ESL), dentists, or maintenance workers with a knowledge of plumbing, electricity, painting and light construction. Placement for tutors/teachers and maintenance workers must be for at least six months; a minimum of one year for dentists and ESL teachers. Conversational Spanish is required.

Volunteers may live at the UPAVIM building, where they receive lunch on weekdays but must otherwise pay for meals and travel expenses.

## United Methodist Volunteers in Mission
159 Ralph McGill Blvd. NE, #305
Atlanta, GA 30308
(404) 659-5060, fax (404) 659-2977
102024.1276@compuserve.com
http://www.gbgm-umc.org/jurisdictions/Volunteers

Projects of the UM Volunteers in Mission support church and community programs. Volunteers placements are available for builders, medical personnel, child care assistants, teachers and counselors. Length of service ranges from one month to one year. Some programs provide room and board. The Volunteers in Mission produces the following publications: the *Handbook for Volunteers in Mission* ($15), a comprehensive guide to preparing and leading a Volunteer in Mission team; and the *Project List* ($2), which includes hundreds of projects currently available in the U.S. and overseas for both teams and individual volunteers.

## United Nations Volunteer Program (UNV)
United Nations Volunteer Office
c/o Peace Corps
1990 K St. NW, 8th floor
Washington, DC 20526
(800) 424-8580, ext. 2243 or (202) 606-3370, fax (202) 606-3298
http://www.peacecorps.gov
or
Postfach 260111, D-53153 Bonn, Germany
(49-228) 815-2000, fax (49-228) 815-2001
enquiry@unv.org
http://www.unv.org

The UNV Program assigns volunteers to United Nations' projects or to government services in UN-member countries. Over 2500 volunteers are currently serving. Projects include humanitarian relief and election-observer missions. Placements last from three weeks to three years. Volunteers are mostly professionals with a graduate degree or a technical diploma plus several years of work experience. Individuals with cross-cultural living experience are preferred. Volunteers must be between the ages of 21 and 65. Volunteers receive a small monthly stipend and international resettlement costs, while the host country provides housing.

## University Research Expeditions Program (UREP)
University of California
Berkeley, CA 94720
(510) 642-6586, fax (510) 642-6791
urep@uclink.berkeley.edu
http://www.mip.berkeley.edu/urep

UREP invites members of the public to join field research expeditions around the globe in ecology, animal behavior studies, archaeology and anthropology. No special experience is necessary. Most expeditions last two to three weeks. Examples of recent expeditions: 1) a survey of manatee populations in Costa Rica to evaluate the impact of ecotourism; 2) a survey of one of the last remaining cloud forests of Ecuador; 3) a study of the impact of human populations on the wetlands of Belize; and 4) a collaborative archaeological excavation of a 17th-century castle in Benin, West Africa. UREP strongly encourages collaborative projects with communities in the host country. Costs range from $700 to $1700 and are tax-deductible. Limited scholarship assistance is available.

## Vellore Christian Medical College Board USA
475 Riverside Dr., Room 243
New York, NY 10115
(212) 870-2640, fax (212) 870-2173
103507.755@compuserve.com

The Board works in collaboration with the 1500-bed, tertiary-care hospital in Vellore, South India. The medical college, college of nursing and 23 allied health departments offer quality education especially in the areas of tropical medicine, leprosy and community health. Volunteers are needed in computer programming, education, health care, community development and social justice. A limited number of elective students are accepted each year. The language of instruction is English. Volunteers pay for their own travel and living expenses.

## Visions in Action
2710 Ontario Rd. NW
Washington, DC 20009
(202) 625-7403, fax (202) 625-2353
visions@igc.apc.org

Visions in Action is a nonprofit organization that sends volunteers to Burkina Faso, Mexico, South Africa, Tanzania, Uganda and Zimbabwe. Volunteers work for one year with nongovernmental organizations in fields such as small business management, health care, journalism, women's issues, the environment, human rights, housing, refugee assistance, family planning, youth and children's services and community development. A program fee of $4000 to $6000 includes housing, insurance, airfare, orientation and overseas support. Visions in Action provides volunteers with detailed information on personal fundraising. Volunteers receive a monthly stipend and in-country assistance.

## Visions International
P.O. Box 220
Newport, PA 17074-0220
(717) 567-7313 or (800) 813-9283; fax (717) 567-7853

Established as a nonprofit organization in 1989, Visions International offers uniquely integrated summer experiences for teenagers. Current program sites are in Alaska, Montana Plains Indian reservations, North Carolina, Dominica, Guadeloupe, the Dominican Republic and the British Virgin Islands. Visions accentuates community service, blending cross-cultural experiences with outdoor adventure. Visions emphasizes coopera-tive living and community-building. Vision's projects always emphasize construction, in addition to working with the young, the elderly, or the handicapped; and working in national parks and wilderness areas. Partici-pants learn carpentry skills from staff carpenters.

Past projects have included construction of housing, schools, medical clinics, youth centers and playgrounds. In North America, recreation opportunities include rock climbing, ice climbing, wilderness backpacking, rafting and horseback riding. Projects in the Caribbean offer swimming, hiking, snorkeling and (in the British Virgin Islands) scuba diving. Visions programs are open to individuals aged 14-18. There is a maximum of 25 students in any program. The staff-to-student ratio is one to four. Four-week sessions are offered in July; and three-week sessions in August. Program costs are $2300 to $3500 depending on the location and length of the program.

## Voluntarios Solidarios
Fellowship of Reconciliation Task Force on Latin America and the Caribbean
995 Market St., Suite 801
San Francisco, CA 94103
(415) 495-6334, fax (415) 495-5628
forlatam@igc.apc.org

Voluntarios Solidarios is a program sponsored by the Fellowship of Reconciliation that places North American volunteers with Latin American and Caribbean groups engaged in nonviolence education, human rights documentation, and organizing and advocacy efforts with the region's poor majority. Possible placements include groups in Bolivia, Brazil, Chile, Ecuador, Nicaragua, Panama and Paraguay. Common activities include translation of publications, support for peace actions, conflict resolution, human welfare service, child care or elderly care and technical assistance in skills such as carpentry, computer operation and recycling. Volunteers must be at least 21 years old and conversant in Spanish or Portuguese. Length of service ranges from three months to two years. The application fee is $50; volunteers are responsible for travel and living expenses.

## Volunteer Optometric Service to Humanity (VOSH International)

505 S. Clay
Taylorville, IL 62568
(217) 824-6152 or (800) 395-8674; fax (217) 824-6176

VOSH brings visual care to needy people throughout the world, particularly in the Third World. Volunteers include ophthalmologists, optometrists and lay assistants. Volunteers serve for one week to one month at locations in Africa, Asia or Latin America. Volunteers pay travel expenses and insurance. Room and board are sometimes provided.

## Volunteers Exchange International (VEI)

International Christian Youth Exchange
134 W. 26th St.
New York, NY 10001
(212) 206-7307, fax (212) 633-9085
vei@igc.apc.org or icyeus@igc.apc.org
http://www.igc.apc.org/vei

VEI is the U.S. committee of the International Christian Youth Exchange, which is headquartered in Berlin and organizes hundreds of exchanges each year. VEI creates opportunities for participants to develop international understanding and sensitivity to social, political and economic realities in the world. VEI coordinates both high-school home-stays and full-time voluntary service placements abroad lasting six months to one year. Programs are available in 30 countries, including Bolivia, Brazil, Colombia, Costa Rica, Ghana, Honduras, India, Kenya, Mexico, Nigeria, and Sierra Leone. Volunteer service opportunities include working with children, the elderly, or the disabled; teaching; environmental projects; community development; culture and arts programs; health care; drug abuse services; and peace work. Volunteers live with host families or in independent settings and earn a modest weekly stipend from the agency to which they are assigned. The cost is $4500 for six-month programs and $5500 for one-year programs. The fee covers international transportation, room and board, orientation in the U.S. and the host country, language training, in-country conferences and evaluations and medical and liability insurance. The age requirement is 18-30; there are no language or academic requirements.

## Volunteers for Peace (VFP)

43 Tiffany Rd.
Belmont, VT 05730-0202
(802) 259-2759, fax (802) 259-2922
vfp@vermontel.com
http://www.vfp.org

VFP was formed to create peaceful relations between nations through voluntary service and international education. VFP is an Executive Committee member of the Coordinating Committee for International Voluntary Service (CCIVS). (See entry in Chapter 7, "Getting More Information".) VFP, serving as a clearing house for volunteers and hosts, recruits North Americans for over 800 International Workcamps in 60 countries in Africa, Asia, Australia, Latin America, Eastern and Western Europe and the former Soviet Union, as well as many regions in the U.S. At each workcamp, 10-20 people from at least four countries live and work together for two to three weeks. Projects are in the fields of construction, restoration, the environment, social services, agriculture and archaeology. Volunteers pay their own travel expenses and a registration fee of $175, which includes room and board.

## Volunteers in Asia

P.O. Box 4543
Stanford, CA 94309
(415) 723-3228, fax (415) 725-1805
via@igc.apc.org
http://www.volasia.org/via_press.html

At the request of Asian institutions, Volunteers in Asia place college undergraduates and graduates in English teaching and English resource positions in China, Indonesia, Laos and Vietnam. Posts for undergraduates range from one summer to a full year; for graduates, one to two years. Accepted applicants must reside in the Santa Cruz or S.F. Bay area to attend a five-month, part-time training program at Stanford University and the University of California, Santa Cruz. Participants pay a fee ranging from $950-$1500, which covers airfare, insurance and housing. During their stay, they receive a stipend for their living expenses.

## Volunteers in Overseas Cooperative Assistance (VOCA)

50 F St. NW, Suite 1075
Washington, DC 20001
(202) 383-4961, fax (202) 783-7204

Established in 1970, VOCA is a nonprofit, international development organization providing short-term, volunteer technical and managerial support to developing and emerging-market countries. Its principal objectives are to enhance the development and economic opportunities of cooperatives and agriculturally-based enterprises, to strengthen democratic institutions, and to promote sound management and conservation of the environment. VOCA operates 24 field offices in Africa, Asia, the Middle East, Latin America and the Caribbean, Central and Eastern Europe and the former Soviet Union. After community-based client organizations delineate their specific requirements to completing a project, VOCA then enlists highly-trained U.S. specialists possessing the precise skills necessary to the project's fulfillment, using its database of over 4000 professionals. Volunteers are commonly placed within eight weeks of a request and project assignments run from two weeks to three months.

## Witness for Peace (WFP)

110 Maryland Ave. NE, Suite 304
Washington, DC 20002
(202) 544-0781, fax (202) 544-1187
witness@w4peace.org
http://www.w4peace.org/witness

Volunteers with WFP, a faith-based, nonviolent, politically-independent organization, live in communities throughout Guatemala, Haiti and Nicaragua, making a renewable two-year commitment. Work includes documenting human rights abuses, studying the effects of U.S. foreign and economic policies, providing socio-political analysis of domestic affairs, facilitating short-term delegations from the U.S., and most importantly, standing with the people in a spirit of nonviolent international cooperation as the means to positive social change. Volunteers must be U.S. citizens, at least 21 years old, Spanish- or Creole-speaking, and committed to a faith-based doctrine of nonviolence. Volunteers are expected to pay costs of round-trip airfare and, if necessary, language school tuition. Volunteers must also attempt to raise $1000 for WFP to help cover living expenses; WFP provides medical expenses, training, room and board, and pays $50 monthly stipend. WFP offers consultation on fund-raising to assure that no qualified candidate is denied for economic reasons.

## World Concern

P.O. Box 33000
Seattle, WA 98133
(206) 546-7201, fax (206) 546-7317
wconcern@crista.org

World Concern is an interdenominational organization that focuses on food production, veterinary care and animal husbandry, water development and primary health care. It has projects and volunteers in East Africa, South and Southeast Asia and Latin America. Volunteers should be motivated to work cross-culturally out of a Christian faith. Those not speaking a native language must attend language school. The minimum commitment is two to three years. World Concern provides volunteers with a modest salary, housing, health insurance, transportation costs and schooling costs for families and children.

## World Council of Churches (WCC)

Youth Office
P.O. Box 2100
150 route de Ferney
1211 Geneva 2
Switzerland
(41-22) 791-6212 or 791-6211; fax (41-22) 791-0361
wcccoe@gn.apc.org

The WCC recruits youth for summer workcamps in Africa, Asia and the Middle East. Volunteers work for 2-4 weeks in activities such as agriculture, road-building and construction. Volunteers, ages 18-32, pay their own travel expenses and are asked to contribute to their living expenses.

## WorldTeach

Harvard Institute for International Development (HIID)
1 Eliot St.
Cambridge, MA 02138-5705
(617) 495-5527 or (800) 4-TEACH-0 (483-2240);

fax (617) 495-1599
info@worldteach.org
http://www.igc.org/worldteach

WorldTeach, a nonprofit organization based at Harvard University, sends volunteers to developing countries. Individuals with a bachelor's degree may teach for one year in Costa Rica, Ecuador, Lithuania, Namibia, Poland, South Africa, Thailand and Vietnam. There is no language requirement. A program fee ranging from $3600 to $4700 covers the cost of international airfare, health insurance, field support, training and administration. WorldTeach provides room and board, and a modest stipend. Additional programs include a six-month nature-guide training program in Mexico (open to college graduates) and an eight-week summer teaching program in Shanghai, China (for graduates and undergraduates).

## YMCA of the USA

71 W. 23rd St., Suite 1904
New York, NY 10010
(212) 727-8800 or (888) IPS-YMCA (477-9622);
fax (212) 727-8814
ips@ymcanyc.org

The YMCA of the USA sponsors two programs for Americans who wish to work or volunteer abroad. The International Camp Counselor Program (ICCP) provides work opportunities in YMCA camps overseas. Americans can volunteer at camps in the Northern Hemisphere (Europe, Asia and the Caribbean) from mid-June to mid-July and in the Southern Hemisphere (Africa, South America, Australia and New Zealand) from the end of December to February. Participants must be 20-30 years old and have previous experience at YMCA camps. They are expected to incorporate their experience into their YMCA work at home. Volunteers pay all international and domestic travel costs and personal expenses while at camp and ICCP provides medical insurance. There is an application fee of $155; however, if ICCP is unable to find a placement, the applicant receives a $100 refund.

YMCA of the USA also has a volunteer program in Europe. Persons over 18 with experience in local YMCAs may work in a European YMCA. Most positions are in Eastern Europe.

# 4
# WORKING IN
# THE U.S. & CANADA

This chapter, published for the first time in this edition, includes a sampling of organizations providing work/volunteer opportunities in development, environment and social justice programs in North America. Many organizations offer programs both in the U.S. and abroad. See the last page of this chapter for a list of groups listed in other chapters that also do work in North America.

## Amnesty International

322 8th Ave.
New York, NY 10001
1-800-AMNESTY
http;//www.igc.apc.org/amnesty/

Amesty International is the world's largest human rights organization. It advocates for the release of prisoners of conscience, for the fair and prompt trial of prisoners, and for an end to torture, executions and disappearances. There are volunteer positions available at the five regional offices in Boston, Atlanta, Chicago, Washington DC and San Francisco. There are also about 400 community groups and 1500 student groups in grade schools, high schools and colleges. Groups get involved in letter-writing, education and public actions. Amnesty will put you in touch with local groups, and will send you information on how to volunteer.

## Association of Community Organization for Reform Now (ACORN)

117 W. Harrison St., #200
Chicago, IL 60605
(312) 939-7488, fax (312) 939-8256
http://www.acorn.org/community

ACORN is a neighborhood-based, multiracial, membership organization of low-income families working on issues such as housing, school reform, redlining, lead poisoning, jobs and living wages. Volunteers work as grassroots organizers in one of 30 cities throughout the U.S. and must commit to one year or more of service. A working knowledge of Spanish is useful, but not required. Volunteers are ginen training and a salary.

## Christmas in April USA

1536 16th St. NW
Washington, DC 20036-1402
(202) 483-9083, fax (202) 483-9081

Founded in 1973, Christmas in April USA is a volunteer organization that, in partnership with communities, rehabilitates the houses of low-income homeowners, particularly the elderly and disabled. Following the American tradition of barn raising, volunteers for Christmas in April observe a National Rebuilding Day, usually on the last Saturday in April. Christmas in April currently serves over 500 cities and towns rehabilitating over 4700 houses every year. By relying on donated materials and volunteers, Christmas in April has become the ninth-largest home-improvement company in the U.S. Christmas in April also promotes the replication and coordination of similar programs throughout the U.S.

### Citizen Action

1730 Rhode Island Ave. NW, Suite 403
Washington, DC 20036
(202) 775-1580, fax (202) 296-4054
Citizenact@aol.com

Citizen Action is the nation's largest nonpartisan consumer and environmental watchdog organization. With three million members in 34 states, Citizen Action fights for increased employment and better-paying jobs; a clean, healthy environment; cheaper and cleaner forms of energy; affordable and quality health care; a system of justice protecting consumers; and a government free from the influence of special-interest groups.

### Earth Island Institute (EII)

300 Broadway, Suite 28
San Francisco, CA 94133-3312
(415) 788-3666, fax (415) 788-7324
earthisland@earthisland.org
http://www.earthisland.org/

Earth Island Institute focuses on critical ecological issues. Among the EII projects that need volunteers are the Atmosphere Alliance which launches ecological initiatives in the Pacific Northwest; Bluewater Network which is fighting global marine pollution from personal watercraft; Rethink Paper Campaign which encourages use of recycled and tree-free papers; and the Southern Rockies Restoration Project which rehabilitates lands in that ecoregion through watershed management and restoration. Projects in California include the Estuary Action Challenge which encourages inner-city students to work to restore habitats of the San Francisco Bay area; Stewards of the Earth which makes presentations on traditional organic agriculture; Urban Habitat Program which cultivates urban multicultural environmental leadership; San Francisco Bay Seal Project which researches and works to conserve the local harbor seals; Wild Alive California which works to protect wildlife in California; and Yosemite Guardian which seeks to protect Yosemite National Park's ecosystems.

## Farmworker Health Services (FHS)
1234 Massachusetts Ave. NW, #C1017
Washington, DC 20005
(202) 347-7377, fax (202) 347-6385

FHS is directed toward the empowerment of migratory and seasonal farmworkers along the U.S. east coast by providing health care, outreach services, preventative health education, and group networking. Volunteers are health professionals of all levels, as well as social workers and others interested in providing outreach services. There is a particular need for nurse practitioners, community and public health nurses, licensed practical nurses and other professionals with specialty certificates. FHS also recruits people in allied health fields, such as medical social workers, nutritionists, health educators, psychologists and physical assistants. Geographic mobility and possession of a car with adequate insurance are required. Volunteers receive a subsistence stipend and must commit for a minimum of one year. Language skills in Spanish, Creole, or Konjobal are helpful.

## Frontiers Foundation/Operation Beaver
2615 Danforth Ave., Suite 203
Toronto, Ontario M4C 1L6, Canada
(416) 690-3930, fax (416) 690-3934

The Frontiers Foundation is a community-development service organization that works in partnership with communities in low-income, rural areas across northern Canada. These locally initiated projects build and improve housing, conduct training programs, and organize recreational and educational activities in this region. Volunteers must be at least 18 years old and available for a minimum of 12 weeks. Skills in carpentry, electrical work and plumbing are preferred for construction projects, while previous social service and experience with children are preferred for recreation and educational projects. While projects run year-round, new volunteers enter the program in April or November. Volunteers for educational projects are needed for longer periods, lasting from the beginning of January to the end of June, or the beginning of September to the end of January. Placements of up to 18 months are possible, provided the volunteer's work is satisfactory after an initial 12-week period. Accommodation, food and travel expenses inside Canada are provided.

**Frontlash**

815 16th St. NW

Washington, DC 20006

(202) 783-3993 or (800) 833-3250, fax (202) 783-3591

youthlabor@aol.com

Frontlash educates students by involving them in labor struggles. Students work with unions organizing campaigns, fighting for an increase in the minimum wage and opposing child labor. Frontlash organizes students on campuses to raise awareness about companies that deprive their workers of the right to organize. Other opportunities include semester and summer internships in Washington, DC, which involve coordination of national campaigns, research and field organizing. Interns and field organizers need not have special experience and may receive a stipend.

**Greenpeace**

Human Resources Department

1436 U St. NW

Washington, DC 20009

(202) 462-1177, fax (202) 462-4507

michael.rodman@green2.greenpeace.org

http://www.greenpeace.org

Greenpeace is an independent campaign organization which uses nonviolent creative confrontation to expose global environmental problems and to force solutions essential to a sustainable and peaceful future. Its campaign priorities are toxic substances, biodiversity and non-proliferation of nuclear arms. Interns are needed to work in one or more of its five divisions, including Campaigns, Development and Media, Public Outreach, Finance and Administration. Internships are available in Atlanta, Chicago, San Francisco, Seattle and Washington, DC. Each intern must attend orientation, which uses publications and videos produced by Greenpeace. Good oral and written communication and expertise in the natural sciences are helpful skills. Many interns develop valuable skills while on the job. No stipends are available.

**Jubilee Partners**

P.O. Box 68

Comer, GA 30629-0068

(706) 783-5131, fax (706) 783-5134

jubileep@igc.apc.org

Jubilee Partners, a Christian service community located on 260 acres of land, provides temporary placement for new refugees needing assistance to learn English and other skills for life in the United States. After a two-month stay at Jubilee, refugees receive assistance from other resettlement agencies. Jubilee invites 10-12 volunteers to live in the community and work in such areas as ESL; preschool child care; gardening; cleaning; and maintenance and construction. Volunteers must be at least 19 years old and willing to do a variety of tasks. They must also be interested in Jubilee's Christian, service and community ideals. There are three volunteer terms each year: January-May, June-August and September-December. Jubilee provides room and board, and a small stipend; transportation and insurance, however, are not provided. Volunteers must attend weekly meetings addressing issues of Christian discipleship (topics include lifestyle, death penalty and war tax resistance).

## Lutheran Volunteer Corps (LVC)

1226 Vermont Ave. NW
Washington, DC 20005
(202) 387-3222, fax (202) 667-0037
lvc_dc.parti@ecunet.org

LVC provides needed staffing to nonprofit organizations in the following areas: direct service, public policy, advocacy, community organizing, health care and education. LVC upholds the ideals of social justice, community living and simplicity. Required qualifications depend upon each placement. Volunteers must be at least 21 years old and have no dependents. Placements are in Baltimore, Chicago, Milwaukee, Minneapolis-St. Paul, Seattle, Tacoma, Wilmington and Washington, DC. Volunteers work for one to two years and live communally in groups of four to seven. Travel, room and board, medical coverage and work-related transportation expenses are covered. Volunteers also receive a small personal stipend. The Lutheran Volunteer Corps is open to people of all faiths.

## Marianist Voluntary Service Communities (MVSC)

P.O. Box 9224
Wright Brothers Branch
Dayton, OH 45409
(937) 229-4630, fax (937) 229-2772
mvsc@saber.udayton.edu

MVSC is a faith-based volunteer program providing services to disadvantaged people in urban areas of Ohio, Kentucky and New York. The program provides services through existing social agencies and offers Christian lay persons an opportunity for personal and spiritual development through service, Christian community and a simple lifestyle. Placements include advocacy, community organizing, day-care, education, health care, housing rehabilitation and programs for women and children, troubled youth and the homeless. MVSC requires a one-year commitment beginning in mid-August, with the option to renew for a second year. Volunteers must be at least 21 years old and single or married without dependents. Student loan deferments can be arranged and Americorps post-service Education Awards are available for certain positions only. Volunteers must be able to pay transportation expenses to and from their assignment; a stipend covers room and board and other living expenses.

## Mercy Corps
Gwynedd Mercy College
P.O. Box 901
Gwynedd Valley, PA 19437-0901
(215) 641-5535, fax (215) 641-5503

Mercy Corps places 45-55 volunteers annually with the Sisters of Mercy of the Americas in serving the poor, sick and uneducated. Mercy Corps empowers volunteers with opportunities for compassionate service, community and spiritual growth. Volunteer placements in the continental U.S. include administrative development, public relations and volunteer coordination; AIDS ministry; child care; community organizing; counseling; dorm moderating; elderly outreach; health care; nursing; ministry to Hispanics, migrant workers and Native Americans; housing programs; services to the physically and mentally challenged; shelter coordination; social work; elementary and high-school teaching, special education and assistant teaching; and occupational, physical and speech therapy. Length of service is one year with the option for a second. Volunteers must be 21 years old, have a high school diploma and undergo a physical examination. Single or married individuals of any denomination are eligible. Some positions require a college degree, certification, or certain type of work experience. Room and board, medical insurance, and a stipend are provided. Transportation to and from the service site are covered; volunteers pay for transportation to Gwynedd Valley for orientation.

## National Student Campaign Against Hunger & Homelessness (NSCAHH)
11965 Venice Blvd. #408
Los Angeles, CA 90066

1-800-NO-HUNGER, ext 324, 310-397-5270 ext 324
fax 310-391-0053

The NSCAHH is a coalition of student-community activists who fight poverty through service programs, education and fundraising. Their annual conference each October brings together hundreds of students, educators and anti-hunger advocates. At their yearly April Hunger Cleanup, campus groups raise funds for anti-poverty groups by getting their friends and relatives to sponsor their volunteer hours at neighborhood work projects like painting shelters, cleaning up playgrounds, or stating community food gardens. NSCAHH can supply volunteers with ideas for organizing a Hunger Cleanup, educating students, increasing community services, building campus coalitions and supporting anti-poverty legislation.

## Passionist Lay Missioners
5700 N. Harlem Ave.
Chicago, IL 60631-2342
(773) 631-6336, fax (773) 631-8059

Passionist Lay Missioners address the immediate and systemic problems of poverty by working with the economically disadvantaged and disenfranchised of Chicago, Cincinnati, Detroit and other cities. Opportunities include placements for social workers, youth workers, advocates for the homeless, teachers and teachers' aides, emergency intervention workers, community organizers, peace and justice advocates, prisoners' rights advocates, child care workers, skilled and semi-skilled tradespeople, counselors, domestic violence workers, clerical workers, care for the elderly and legal aides. Positions begin in August and last for one year with an option to renew. Volunteers live in a communal setting, usually in a low-income, inner-city neighborhood. They live a simple lifestyle and explore connections between work, community, faith and social justice. Volunteers pay for their own transportation to their orientation in August. Room and board, health insurance, a monthly stipend of $100 and transportation during the year are provided. Applicants must be at least 21 years old, have some college education or practical work experience and be willing to engage in spiritual reflection.

## Rainforest Action Network (RAN)
450 Sansome St., Suite 700
San Francisco, CA 94111
(415) 398-4404, fax (415) 398-2732

helpran@ran.org
rags@ran.org
http://www.ran.org/ran/

Rainforest Action Network works to protect the earth's rainforests and the rights of their inhabitants through education, grassroots organizing and nonviolent direct action. Past campaigns include the 1987 Burger King boycott to stop cutting down rainforests to raise cheap beef. RAN's current education and advocacy programs include the Wood-Use Reduction and Boycott Mitsubishi campaigns, the Amazon and Protect-An-Acre programs, International Information Clearinghouse and World Rainforest Week. Many internship opportunities are available in media operations, database coordination, campaign coordination and administration, information and development assistance and executive administration. Requirements include basic Macintosh computer skills, a passion to save the environment and a commitment to work at least 12 hours a week for three months. RAN reimburses interns for local commuting expenses.RAN also has associated groups of community- and campus-based organizations called Rainforest Action Groups (RAGs) which are in need of volunteers. There are 125 RAGs in the U.S. and throughout the world that are engaged in education, issue-oriented campaigns and fund-raising.

## Union Summer

815 16th St. NW
Washington, DC 20006
(202) 639-6220 or (800) 952-2550, fax 408-0303
unionsmr@aol.com
http://www.aflcio.org

Union Summer is an internship sponsored by the AFL-CIO. Interns support union campaigns in a number of sites across the U.S. Specific activities include communicating with workers at home and at work, coordinating demonstrations and actions, and helping organize new unions. Participants must be at least 18 years old and have an interest in labor organizing. Union Summer provides interns with housing and local transportation in addition to a weekly stipend.

## Ursuline Companions in Mission

College Center, Room 155
College of New Rochelle
New Rochelle, NY 10805
(914) 654-5270, fax (914) 654-5554

Christian volunteers are placed in inner-city and rural service sites in the U.S. to provide education, social service, pastoral ministry, youth ministry, child care, poverty relief services, ministry to the elderly and prison or detention-center ministries. Volunteers must be at least 21 years old and possess skills compatible with the needs of specific ministries. Short-term volunteers (serving less than six months) must cover transportation expenses and medical insurance. All costs for long-term volunteers (including up to $400 in transportation expenses) are paid by the program. All companions are offered an orientation the summer before their service and a retreat at mid-year.

## U.S. Public Interest Research Group (US PIRG)
218 D St. SE
Washington, DC 20003
(202) 546-9707, fax (202) 546-2461
uspirg@pirg.org
http://www.pirg.org/pirg/

US PIRG is a leading environmental and consumer watch-dog groups. Since 1983, US PIRG has exposed corporate abuses and government neglect, uncovered numerous examples of political hypocrisy, won lawsuits and court settlements against polluters, forced manufacturers to recall unsafe products, and helped pass laws protecting clean air and water. Internships are available at PIRG offices in 25 states. Interns conduct research on public policy and prepare reports, help coordinate media events, participate in grassroots campaigns, monitor Congressional legislation and the actions of federal agencies, and help administer the office. Qualifications include strong research and writing skills. Although internships are unpaid, students may get academic credit for participating.

# # # # #

The following groups also have programs in the U.S. and are listed in other sections: Bikes Not Bombs, Brethren Volunteer Services, Casa de los Amigos, Catholic Network of Volunteer Service, Christian Peacemaker Teams, Christian Service International, Global Volunteers, Institute for Cultural Affairs, Involvement Volunteers Association, Peace Brigades International, Peacework, Plenty International, Ponape Agriculture and Trade School, Service Civil International, SMA Lay Missionaries, United Methodist Volunteers in Mission, Visions International and Volunteers in Mission.

# 5
# STUDY
# OPPORTUNITIES

The following list is just a sprinkling of the thousands of opportunities to study overseas. For more information on study opportunities, see the suggestions listed in Chapter 7, "Getting More Information." You should also contact the following organizations:

**Council on International Educational Exchange (CIEE)**, 205 E. 42nd St., New York, NY 10017-5706, (212) 822-2695 or (888) COUNCIL, fax (212) 822-2689, http://www.ciee.org/

**Institute of International Education (IIE)**, 809 U.N. Plaza, New York, NY 10017, (212) 883-8200

**National Association for Foreign Student Affairs**, 1875 Connecticut Ave. NW, Suite 1000, 20009, (202) 462-4811

## American Field Service Intercultural Programs (AFS)

198 Madison Ave., 8th floor
New York, NY 10016
(212) 299-9000, (800) 876-2376, or (800) AFS-INFO (237-4636);
fax (212) 299-9090
afsinfo@afs.org
http://www.afs.org/usa

Celebrating 50 years of service in 1997, the AFS is the most experienced high-school international exchange program in the world. AFS programs help students learn to deal with diversity and understand different cultures. A nonprofit organization, AFS offers more than 100 summer, semester, and full-year programs in 46 countries. In addition, AFS's Interim Pre-College programs are available for high-school graduates wishing to take time off before going to college. AFS also seeks families to host students from abroad. (Also see entry in Chapter 3.)

## Centro Tlahuica de Lenguas e Intercambio Cultural (Tlahuica Center for Language and Cultural Exchange)

Apartado Postal 1-201
62000 Cuernavaca, Morelos
Mexico
(52-73) 12-17-08, fax (52-73) 12-67-18
cetlalic@laneta.apc.org
http://www.laneta.apc.org:80/cetlalic

CETLALIC offers intensive instruction in Spanish and exposure to Mexican culture, with programs that analyze the present situation in

Mexico and Central America. Small participatory classes are available at all levels, and meet on weekday mornings. The method of teaching follows the ideas of popular educator Paulo Freire, in which teacher and student together explore the complexities of language and culture. Students exercise their Spanish skills through the cultural programming offered in the afternoon and evening. Topics addressed include politics, ecology, indigenous cultures, women, education, popular movements, the arts, religion, the economy, human rights, independent journalism and unions. Group instruction costs $125 per week; private instruction is $200. The registration fee is $70 and remains valid for two years. Limited financial aid is available. For an additional fee, CETLALIC makes arrangements for students to room and board with families. It is the only school in Cuernavaca to offer gay/lesbian-friendly housing. The school can also arrange for apartment accommodations or recommend a hotel.

### Council on International Educational Exchange (CIEE)
205 E. 42nd St.
New York, NY 10017-5706
(212) 822-2600, fax (212) 822-2799
info@ciee.org

The CIEE is a membership organization of over 300 colleges and institutions throughout the country. It coordinates dozens of undergraduate study abroad opportunities and some graduate study opportunities. Programs are in Central Asia, Latin America and the Caribbean, as well as Europe. Programs may last for one summer, semester, or a full academic year. The Council also publishes books and guides listing universities throughout the U.S. that have overseas programs. (Also see entry in Chapter 3 and Chapter 7.)

### Eco-Escuela de Español
c/o Conservation International
1015 18th St. NW, Suite 1000
Washington, DC 20036
(202) 973-2264, fax (202) 887-5188
m.sister@conservation.org
http://www.conservation.org

A joint venture of Conservation International and the community of San Andrés in the Petén in Guatemala, the Eco-Escuela de Español offers students a unique educational opportunity by combining intensive Spanish-language instruction with hands-on environmental education. The school's mission is to immerse students in the language, culture, and ecology of the Petén, an area renowned for its tropical forests and ancient Maya ruins. One-on-one language instruction is tailored to meet the needs of students at all levels. Classroom interaction is combined with field-based experiences, such as ecological activities or volunteer opportunities. The cost per week is $110, which includes 20 hours of classes, and room and board with local families. The registration fee is $10. Classes begin every Monday.

## Escuela de Español "Juan Sisay" (Juan Sisay Spanish Language School)

3465 Cedar Valley Ct.

Smyrna, GA 30080

(770) 436-6283

or

15 Avenida 8-38, Zona 1

Quetzaltenango, Guatemala

The Juan Sisay Spanish Language School is a nonprofit educational collective, combining intensive Spanish instruction with community-service projects in order to give students a deeper understanding of the current issues Guatemalans are facing. Language courses are offered year-round, emphasizing Spanish grammar, and meeting five hours per day for five days a week. One-on-one instruction is also available. Students determine the length of their study, ranging from a single day to several months. Additional activities include weekly sessions in political, historical, and social analysis. The school also coordinates local community projects, including reforestation and work in an orphanage. Tuition is $135 per week from June 1 to August 15, $110 for the remainder of the year. This includes accommodations; typically the school places students with local families.

## Escuela de Español "Melida Anaya Montes" (Melida Anaya Montes Spanish Language School)

c/o Committee in Solidarity with the People of El Salvador

P.O. Box 1801

New York, NY 10159

(212) 229-1290, fax (212) 645-6657

cispesnatl@igc.apc.org

or

Urbanización Padilla Cuellar

Pasaje Los Pinos, #17

San Salvador, El Salvador
(011-503) 225-0076, fax (011-503) 225-0076
cis@nicarao.apc.org

The Melida Anaya Montes Spanish Language School operates year-round. Students are placed in small classes meeting every weekday morning (i.e., 20 hours a week). Students spend afternoons and weekends participating in cultural and political programs. These may include visits to artisan cooperatives; participation in cultural workshops; language discussions with Salvadorans studying English; and meetings with leaders of the women's movement, student organizations, Christian base communities, labor and peasant unions, and the Farabundo Martí National Liberation Front (FMLN). Students are housed with families working towards social change in El Salvador. The cost is $177.50 per week which includes housing, two meals per day, materials, instruction, and political programs. Although it is not required, students are encouraged to raise additional funds for material aid to support grassroots organizations such as the Melida Anaya Montes Women's Movement.

## Friends World Program
239 Montauk Hwy.
Southampton, NY 11968
(516) 287-8465, fax (516) 287-8463
fw@southampton.liunet.edu
http://www.southampton.liunet.edu/academic/fr_world/program.htm

The Friends World Program is a four-year, coeducational, international college offering an accredited B.A. in interdisciplinary studies. It encourages students to pursue their own academic agendas while developing essential skills. With eight centers around the world, students usually spend their first year in the U.S. and the following three abroad at one of the program's other centers, which are located in China, Costa Rica, England, India, Israel, Japan, and Kenya.

## Global Exchange Language Programs
2017 Mission St., #303
San Francisco, CA 94110
(415) 255-7296, fax (415) 255-7498
gx-info@globalexchange.org
http://www.globalexchange.org

Global Exchange, in conjunction with the University of Havana and the Latin American Faculty of Social Science (FLACSO), provides an alternative and comprehensive way to learn Spanish and understand Cuba's vibrant culture. The Spanish Language Program offers courses at all levels; classroom instruction is held weekday mornings. Special weekly meetings with Cuban specialists focus on the economy, politics, social programs, cooperative farming, women, film and arts, Afro-Cuban culture, alternative energy, public health and alternative medicine. There are opportunities on weekends to to travel to the countryside or beach. Students must stay for a minimum of two weeks, and course extensions of an additional two or four weeks are available. The cost of a two-week program is $1200, which includes airfare from Cancún, Mexico, day trips, cultural programs, accommodations, language instruction and certificate from the University of Havana, two meals per day, and visa fees.

GX also offers Spanish instruction at Mar de Jade, a cross-cultural, oceanfront retreat located in a fishing village 60 miles north of Puerto Vallarta, Mexico. Students can vacation, learn Spanish, and/or work in the community health clinic. Language classes are small and personalized; all teachers are native speakers.

Another Spanish school supported by GX is located in Quetzaltenango, Guatemala. Students learn Spanish in the unique atmosphere of the Pop Wuj Center. The school combines a high quality of teaching with humanitarian objectives. Students are offered personalized instruction and one-on-one conversational practice with educated native speakers. If they wish to become more involved in the community, students may participate in work projects and live with a Guatemalan family.

## Institute for Central American Development Studies (ICADS)
Dept. 826, P.O. Box 025216
Miami, FL 33102-5216
or
Apartado 3-2070, Sabanilla
San Jose, Costa Rica
(506) 225-0508, fax (506) 234-1337
icads@netbox.com

Based in Costa Rica, ICADS is a center for study, research, and analysis of Central American issues in such areas as economic development, agriculture, women's issues, and the environment. In addition to its Spanish program, ICADS offers semester-abroad academic programs during the fall and spring and a shorter summer session. Students are from all age groups, educational levels, and occupations. The program, an intensive five hours per day for five days a week, is geared to the individual abilities and needs of each participant. Students live with Costa Rican families. The total cost for the intensive program is approximately $1150 for the first month, with a 10% discount thereafter. Free internship placements in grassroots organzations are available.

## The International Partnership for Service-Learning

815 2nd Ave., Suite 315
New York, NY 10017-4594
(212) 986-0989, fax (212) 986-5039
pslny@aol.com
http://www.studyabroad.com/psl/

The International Partnership for Service-Learning is a grouping of accredited universities and service organizations providing opportunities for students to combine formal studies with an international/intercultural experience through community service. Semester, full-year, summer and intersession programs are available in the Czech Republic, Ecuador, England, France, India, Israel, Jamaica, Mexico, the Philippines, Scotland, and (in the U.S.) South Dakota. Students study at accredited colleges in their host country and academic credit is granted from their home college. Service opportunities include teaching, health care, and community development. High-school graduates, college undergraduates and recent graduates, and in-service professionals are eligible. In September 1997, the Partnership will inaugurate the Master of Arts in International Service program. Offered in cooperation with the Universidad Autónoma de Guadalajara (Mexico), the University of Technology (Kingston, Jamaica), and the Roehampton Institute of the University of Surrey (London), the program will prepare participants for professional careers in public- and private-sector relief and development organizations. For regular programs, costs range from $3800 to $7700; for the Master's degree program, costs are $28,500.

## International Student Exchange Program (ISEP)

3222 N St. NW, Suite 400
Washington, DC 20007-2849
(202) 965-0550, fax (202) 965-0405
isep@guvax.georgetown.edu

ISEP arranges one-to-one exchanges of college and graduate students between U.S. and international institutions—currently, the program involves 36 other countries. Participants must be regularly-enrolled students in good academic standing and nominated by an ISEP-member institution. Study sites include Africa, Asia, the South Pacific, Central and South America, and Western and Eastern Europe. Costs are variable, depending on the individual home institution.

## International Youth Leadership Fund (IYLF)
10 E. 87th St.
New York, NY 10128
(201) 798-0256
sw179@columbia.edu

The IYLF provides funding for programs focusing on education, training and careers in the international sector. IYLI seeks to increase the number of people of color entering international careers.

IYLF's Summer Fellowship Program is a month-long study program conducted in Africa. Students explore cities and villages, markets and museums, and live in both urban and rural settings. They conduct research projects, meet with other youth and interact with professionals in business, international development, government, and education. Past programs have taken place in Egypt, the Gambia, Ghana, Morocco, and Senegal. African-American and Latino high-school students from across the nation are eligible to participate. The cost of the program is $2700 and includes airfare (from New York City), lodging, ground transportation, meals, entrance fees, and other expenses. Participants must pay for passports, inoculations, and personal expenses. IYLF also offers one-week immersion programs in Spanish-language instruction, conducted during the winter break in Latin America. Past programs have taken place in Mexico and the Dominican Republic. Only IYLI Fellows are eligible to participate.

## La Hermandad Educativa
Apartado Postal 114
Quezaltenango, Guatemala
(011-502) 763-1061, fax (011-502) 765-2140
plqe@nicarao.apc.org
or
915 Cole St., Suite 363
San Francisco, CA 94117-4315
(800) 963-9889, fax (800) 963-9889
lea@itsa.ucsf.edu
http://www.infoserve.net/hermandad/hermandad.htm

La Hermandad Educativa is a nonprofit consortium of Spanish-language schools in Guatemala including the Proyecto Lingüístico Quetzalteco de Español and the Proyecto Lingüístico "Educación para Todos" (both in Quetzaltenango), and the Proyecto Lingüístico de Español y Mam (in Todos Santos). The goals of the Hermandad are to offer affordable, quality Spanish-language instruction to foreign visitors; to promote decent-paying jobs; and to generate income supporting local development projects. All three schools offer intensive one-on-one instruction lasting five hours per day. Students are encouraged to immerse themselves in Guatemalan culture by living with local families. Daily activities include conferences, field trips, films, and discussions about the culture, history, and political and social reality in Guatemala. The schools are open year-round, classes beginning every Monday. In Quetzaltenango, the cost (covering tuition, room and board, materials, and daily activities) is $120 per week in September-May and $150 per week in June-August. In Todos Santos, the cost is $100 per week year-round.

## People to People International
501 E. Armour Blvd.
Kansas City, MO 64109-2200
(816) 531-4701, fax (816) 561-7502
ptpi@cctr.umkc.edu
http://cei.haag.umkc.edu/ptp

People to People International, with the University of Missouri, Kansas City, co-sponsors the Collegiate and Professional Studies Program, offering travel seminars on various topics. Seminars last for two to five weeks in June; additional ones may be held during winter break in December. Topics include international business and economics, international relations, literature, comparative education, health care and social services, and public policy. Each course visits two to three cities in the United Kingdom, Western Europe, or Eastern Europe. Students visit important businesses, agencies, and schools, meeting interactively with top executives and officials. Students in the program may earn three to six hours of undergraduate or graduate credit. Costs range between $2200 and $2500 per course, which covers tuition for three credit hours, all accommodations and surface group travel, admission fees to events, sightseeing tours, and some meals including continental breakfasts. Airfare is not included.

## Rotary Youth Exchange Program
2104 Silver Ln.
Willow Street, PA 17584

(717) 464-3401 or (888) ROTARYX (768-2799);
fax (717) 464-0214
yep7450@redrose.net

The Rotary Youth Exchange Program is an exchange program for high-school students to more than 45 countries. Interested students must be between 15 1/2 and 18 1/2 on the 1st of September in the year they participate. Students in the top third of their class who possess good communication skills are preferred. Participants spend one year in another country, live with three to four host families, attend public school, are hosted by a local Rotary Club, have an assigned counselor, and receive a monthly allowance of $50 to $75. Participants must pay for the cost of their visa, passport, and travel to their assigned country. There is an application fee of $50 and a program fee of $450 which includes orientation and activities, processing, name tags and business cards. Some countries may have an additional insurance fee of up to $440. While the participant is away, his or her family must be willing to host a student from another country for three to six months. Applications are accepted through the 31st of December for departure in the following July or August.

## School for International Training (SIT)
Kipling Rd.
P.O. Box 676
Brattleboro, VT 05302-0676
(802) 257-7751 or (800) 451-4465; fax (802) 258-3500
admissions.sit@worldlearning.org
http://www.worldlearning.org/sit.html

The School for International Training offers international programs for undergraduate and graduate degrees, as well as short-term training programs in NGO management and leadership. Students in SIT's undergraduate degree program, the World Issues Program, focus on one of the following study areas: peace, social and economic development, community studies, and the environment. SIT also offers semester-abroad programs in over 45 countries for university undergraduates. The Master's Program in Intercultural Management offers three areas of concentration: sustainable development, training and human resource development, and international education. The Master of Arts in Teaching (MAT) program offers concentrations in teaching French, Spanish, and English as a second language, and an Internationalist program in cooperation with the Peace Corps. All degree programs combine classroom teaching and practical field experience with internships in the U.S. and around the world. Scholarships are also available from SIT.

SIT, in association with the Organisation of Rural Associations for Progress in Zimbabwe and the Bangladesh Rural Advancement Committee, founded the Global Partnership for NGO Studies, Education and Training. Global Partnership programs are designed for current and future NGO leaders. Participants have the option to pursue certificates, diplomas, undergraduate degrees or graduate degrees.

## Volunteers Exchange International (VEI)

134 W. 26th St.

New York, NY 10001

(212) 206-7307, fax (212) 633-9085

vei@igc.apc.org or icyeus@igc.apc.org

http://www.igc.apc.org/vei

VEI is the U.S. committee of the International Christian Youth Exchange, which is headquartered in Berlin and organizes hundreds of exchanges each year. VEI coordinates high-school homestays in 30 countries. Participants live with families and attend secondary school in their host country. The cost is $4500 for six-month programs and $5500 for one-year programs. The fee covers international transportation, room and board, orientation in the U.S. and the host country, language training, in-country conferences and evaluations, and medical insurance. Age requirement is 16-18 years; there are no language or academic requirements.

## World Studies Program

Office of Admissions

Marlboro College

Marlboro, VT 05344

(802) 257-4333 or (800) 343-0049; fax (802) 257-4154

admissions@marlboro.edu

http://www.marlboro.edu/

Marlboro College (in association with the School for International Training) offers the World Studies Program, a four-year course of study which combines the best traditions of liberal arts education and international studies with a working internship in a foreign culture lasting six to eight months. In choosing the country of their internship, students gain firsthand experiences living and working with people of other cultures while acquiring proficiency in a foreign language.

# 6
# SOCIALLY
# RESPONSIBLE
# TRAVEL

In this chapter you will find a variety of groups that organize tours with a focus on environmental, development, cultural or political issues. While we cannot vouch for every group listed, we have tried to include groups that put visitors in direct contact with local people and foster a respect and appreciation for other cultures.

## Adventure Associates

P.O. Box 16304
Seattle, WA 98116
(206) 932-8352, fax (206) 938-2654
advntrassc@aol.com

Adventure Associates offer ecologically and culturally sensitive trips worldwide. Each trip is designed to support local economies while minimizing its impact on the local environment and culture. Destinations include East Africa, Morocco, Indonesia, Nepal, New Zealand, Costa Rica, Ecuador and the Galapagos, Copper Canyon in Mexico, Greece and the Pacific Northwest (including Alaska). Groups are small (typically eight to ten people) and are guided by local experts. Adventure Associates produce a free annual brochure that provides a full listing and description of programs.

## African American Studies Program (AASP)

19 S. La Salle St., Suite 301
Chicago, IL 60603
(312) 443-0929, fax (312) 684-6967

The AASP sponsors one- to two-week cultural study tours to Benin, Ethiopia, Ghana, Kenya, Senegal, Tanzania, Togo and Zimbabwe. Groups visit educational and cultural sites, meeting faculty and administrators, with additional time for individual sight-seeing. The AASP also conducts two- to three-week programs in Cameroon, Egypt, the Ivory Coast, Mali and South Africa. Tour themes may include education, slavery, the role of women and traditional medicine. Tour costs range from $1000 to $4000, including airfare.

## Amazonia Expeditions

18500 Gulf Blvd., #201
Indian Shores, FL 33785
(800) 262-9669, fax (813) 360-8007

Amazonia Expeditions takes groups of 2-20 people to the Peruvian Amazon; trips are organized year-round. Trips of eight days cost $1095 (not including airfare), although longer trips are also possible. A part of their proceeds may go towards conservation efforts in the Tamshiyaru-Tahuayo Preserve, an oral history project to conserve local traditions, or small village development efforts.

## American Council for International Studies (ACIS)
19 Bay State Rd.
Boston, MA 02215
(617) 236-2051, fax (617) 236-4703
http://www.aifs.org
Founded in 1978, ACIS annually organizes high-quality educational travel programs for approximately 30,000 U.S. high school students and teachers. ACIS coordinates one- to four-week educational trips in Africa, China, Australia, Europe, Mexico and the Americas. ACIS also coordinates campus and home-stay programs for the international summer study programs, providing participants with a more comprehensive educational learning experience. For interested student or special-interest groups, ACIS can develop custom-designed special educational travel programs.

## Backroads
801 Cedar St.
Berkeley, CA 94710-1800
(510) 527-1555 or (800) 462-2848; fax (510) 527-1444
goactive@backroads.com
http://www.backroads.com
Backroads offers 150 different bicycling, hiking and multi-sport trips worldwide. Trips last 5-15 days and cost from $749 to $4295. Destinations include Argentina, Bali, Chile, China, Costa Rica, the Czech Republic, Ecuador and the Galapagos, South Africa and Thailand. All accommodations are included in the price and range from campsites to luxurious chateaus. Catalogs of bicycling, hiking and multi-sport vacations are available upon request.

## Bicycle Africa
International Bicycle Fund
4887 Columbia Dr. South P7
Seattle, WA 98108-1919

(206) 628-9314, fax (206) 767-0848
intlbike@scn.org
http://intlbike.home.ml.org/homepage.html
The International Bicycle Fund promotes bicycle transport, economic development, international understanding and safety education. Bicycle Africa sponsors unique two- to four-week long cultural and educational bicycle tours in Benin, Burkina Faso, Cameroon, Eritrea, Ethiopia, the Gambia, Ghana, Kenya, Malawi, Mali, Senegal, Tanzania, Togo, Tunisia, Uganda and Zimbabwe. Participants explore areas seldom visited by tours and rarely covered in the news. Cross-cultural interaction is extensive. The cycling is moderate with occasional challenging sections, and the average daily distance is 40 miles. Participants do not need extensive bicycle-touring experience, but should be healthy, physically fit and familiar with cycling. Costs range from $1000 to $2000, not including airfare.

**Bike-Aid**
Overseas Development Network (ODN)
333 Valencia Street, Suite 330
San Francisco, CA 94103
(415) 431-4480 or (800) RIDE-808 (743-3808); fax (415) 431-5953
odn@igc.apc.org
http://www.igc.apc.org/odn/
Bike-Aid is a national nonprofit organization dedicated to raising funds for and awareness about global grassroots problems of poverty and social injustice. Each summer since 1986, six Bike-Aid teams of 20 cyclists set off from Seattle, Portland, San Francisco, Montreal and Chapel Hill, NC and bike across the United States. All routes converge for a finale and organizing day in Washington, DC. Along the way, cyclists meet with community activists in homeless shelters, farmers' cooperatives and environmental action groups. Bike-Aid participants learn and share knowledge about community issues around the world. Interested individuals can participate as cyclists, community hosts, or as office volunteers.

**BorderLinks**
710 E. Speedway
Tucson, AZ 85719
(520) 628-8263, fax (520) 740-0242
borderlinks@igc.apc.org
BorderLinks is an ecumenical program that seeks to raise conscious-ness about border issues through experiential education by offering travel

seminars along the Mexico-U.S. border. Its focus includes such issues as refugees and immigration, free trade, the environment, economic justice and U.S.-Mexico relations. The length of a seminar varies depending on the group participating. The trip cost of $50 per day includes all programming, lodging, transportation and meals.

## Casa de los Amigos
Service and Education Project
Ignacio Mariscal 132
06030 Mexico, D.F.
Mexico
(52-5) 705-0521 or 705-0646; fax (52-5) 705-0771
amigos@laneta.apc.org

Casa de los Amigos is a Quaker center of hospitality, volunteer service and cross-cultural dialogue in the heart of Latin America's largest urban megalopolis. The Service and Education Project offers one- to two-week seminars focusing on a specific social concern. Themes include democratic struggles and urban popular movements, women and gender, poverty and the informal sector economy and the urban megalopolis and its environmental impact. Activities include several days working on a community project, field trips to local service organizations, guest lectures, visits with local communities and group reflection. Seminars are limited to 10-12 participants and can be arranged for private groups. Open-registration seminars are scheduled for most months of the year. Fees of $35 per day cover lodging, local transportation, most meals, donations to host organizations and materials for the work project. (Also see entry in Chapter 3, "Working in the Third World")

## CEDAM International
1 Fox Rd.
Croton-on-Hudson, NY 10520
(914) 271-5365, fax (914) 271-4723

CEDAM International (an acronym for Conservation, Education, Diving, Archeology, Museums) is a 30-year old, member-supported, nonprofit organization specializing in scuba-diving expeditions. Members can participate in one- or two-week research trips led by scientists. Expeditions include reef surveys, fish counts and animal behavior studies. Upcoming CEDAM study sites include the Red Sea, Papua New Guinea, the Bahamas, Little Cayman, Venezuela and Hawaii. Costs range from $1500 to $3000.

## Center for Cuban Studies
124 W. 23rd St.
New York, NY 10011
(212) 242-0559, fax (212) 242-1937
cubanctr@igc.apc.org

The Center sponsors numerous trips to Cuba every year. Each tour has a specific focus, such as health care, film, religion, education, or the economic system. Due to U.S. Treasury Department restrictions on travel to Cuba, trips are limited to journalists and professionals of various fields. Prices usually range from $800 to $1200 for seven- and ten-day trips.

## Center for Global Education
Augsburg College
2211 Riverside Ave.
Minneapolis, MN 55454
(612) 330-1159 or (800) 299-8889; fax (612) 330-1695
globaled@augsburg.edu
http://www.augsburg.edu/global

The Center for Global Education sponsors educational travel seminars of 7-21 days to southern Africa, the Asia/Pacific region, Mexico and Central America. These reality tours introduce participants to important social, economic and political issues in the Third World, bringing North Americans face to face with individuals and communities struggling for freedom, justice and human dignity. In addition to hosting its own trips, the Center plans travel seminars for church, community and professional organizations. Depending on the length and destination of each trip, costs range from $1000 to $4500, including airfare.

## Centro Tlahuica de Lenguas e Intercambio Cultural (CETLALIC)
## (Tlahuica Center for Language and Cultural Exchange)
Apartado Postal 1-201
62000 Cuernavaca, Morelos
Mexico
(52-73) 12-17-08, fax (52-73) 12-67-18
cetlalic@laneta.apc.org
http://www.laneta.apc.org:80/cetlalic

CETLALIC sponsors four-week travel programs to southern Mexico and Central America. The purpose of the programs is to create bridges of solidarity and understanding between individuals and groups from different cultures. After one week of classes and orientation in Cuernavaca participants travel various sites, meeting directly with grassroot organizations and indigenous groups. Side trips to the beach, archaeological sites and museums, and participation in local fiestas and cultural events are also included. Travel programs cost $1100 to $1500, including all registration fees. (Also see entry in Chapter 5, "Study Opportunities")

## Committee in Solidarity with the People of El Salvador (CISPES)

P.O. Box 1801
New York, NY 10159
(212) 229-1290, fax (212) 645-6657
cispesnatl@igc.apc.org

CISPES organizes two to three delegations to El Salvador per year. Delegations usually last for one to two weeks and the cost ranges from $1000 to $1500—this includes airfare and in-country costs such as housing, transportation, food and translation. Delegates meet with labor unions, feminist organizations, grassroots organizers, youth organizations, groups educating about AIDS, environmental organizations, art and cultural associations. Delegates may aalso have the opportunity to participate in hands-on work in development projects, accompany organizers out in the field, attend marches and rallies, and participate in workshops and exchanges between U.S. and Salvadoran organizers. Delegations are open to all who have a commitment to social and economic justice.

## Companion Community Development Alternatives (CoCoDA)

609 E. 29th St.
Indianapolis, IN 46205-4199
(317) 920-8643, fax (317) 920-8649
cocodaindy@igc.apc.org

CoCoDA is a nonprofit organization which promotes "Companionship in Development" among communities in the U.S. and Latin America. CoCoDA coordinates work/study/ecotourism delegations to El Salvador, highlighted by community visits which provide an in-depth introduction to social and economic development efforts, placed within the national and historical context of El Salvador. All delegations aim to support in some way the development initiatives visited. Trips tend to be two to three weeks in length and happen throughout the year. Organizations and groups are welcome to tailor-design trips with CoCoDA staff. Cost of participation on a delegation generally ranges from $1200 to $1500 per person, which includes airfare.

## Costa Rica Study Tours

1182 Hornbeam Rd.

Sabina, OH 45169

(513) 382-2869, fax (513) 382-2869

Costa Rica Study Tours provide a unique look at Costa Rica. On most tours five nights are spent near San Jose (the capital) and five nights are spent at Monteverde, a Quaker settlement established in 1951. Although the conditions are rugged, the tour can be a rewarding experience, even for those with physical limitations. Costs range from $995 to $1195 per person, depending on accommodations and other options. Some tours also go to Nicaragua.

## Cross-Cultural Solutions

965 Stunt Rd.

Calabasas, CA 91302

(818) 222-8300 or (800) 380-4777; fax (818) 222-8315

ccsmailbox@aol.com

http://emol.org/emol/projectindia

Cross-Cultural Solutions offers the "Saheli" Women's Tour of India, which focuses on the condition of women. While traveling with a noted leader in Indian women's rights, participants will meet a wide range of women—learning firsthand about their fascinating experiences. The tour last for three weeks and accommodations are in three- or four-star hotels. The fee of $3500 covers all India-based expenses such as lodging, meals and transportation. Airfare is not included. (Also see entry in Chapter 3, "Working in the Third World")

## EarthStewards Network

P.O. Box 10697

Bainbridge Island, WA 98110

(206) 842-7986, fax (206) 842-8918

earthsteward@igc.apc.org

http://www.earthstewards.org/peacetrees

The purpose of the EarthStewards Network is to develop and support simple, effective and innovative models for global change. One section of the Network, the Middle East Citizen Diplomacy program, sends ten delegations to Israel, the West Bank, Gaza and Jordan. As part of the project, participants collect oral histories from both Israelis and Palestinians; through active listening, they discover ways to promote local efforts towards peace. In the Network's tree-planting program, called PeaceTrees, people from around the world meet and discuss large-scale problems concering the environment, human rights and economics. Destinations vary from year to year—past ones have included Vietnam and, in the U.S., Oakland and Salt Lake City. Both prgrams last about three weeks. Costs are $1500 for the Middle East delegations and $200 to $2500 for the tree-planting projects; airfare is included.

## Earthwatch
680 Mt. Auburn St., Box 9104
Watertown, MA 02272
(617) 926-8200 or (800) 776-0188; fax (617) 926-8532
info@earthwatch.org
http://www.earthwatch.org
　　Earthwatch supports scholarly field research by finding volunteers to work with scientists on 160 research expeditions in 50 countries around the world. Volunteers attend projects for a period of one to three weeks and aid scientists in all aspects of their research. Previous projects have included an ecological study of Lake Naivasha in Kenya, a maternal health study in Nepal, a rainforest ecology study in Costa Rica, an excavation at ancient Carthage in Tunisia and a nutrition study in Zimbabwe. Costs range from $500 to $2500 plus airfare. No special skills are needed.

　　Earthwatch offers college credit through Drexel University. Earthwatch also provides intern and volunteer opportunities in staffing its Watertown (Boston), Massachusetts office.

## Friends Witness in Nicaragua
130 19th Ave. SE
St. Petersburg, FL 33705-2810
(813) 821-2428, fax (941) 355-8193
rpaine@igc.apc.org or stillmana@aol.com
or
El Centro de los Amigos
Apartado 5391
Managua, Nicaragua
(505-2) 66-32-16 or 66-09-84
　　Friends Witness Trips give participants an overview of Nicaragua's

culture, politics and development situation. Participants visit several development projects and meet organizers, farmers, teachers, health workers, students and artisans. Each tour is limited to six people and costs $350, which includes accommodations at Quaker House in Managua, transportation to selected sites, translations and meals.

## Genesis II

Apartado 655
7050 Cartago
Costa Rica
(011-506) 381-0739, fax (011-506) 551-0070

Genesis II seeks to preserve the Costa Rican tropical forest, engaging in a broad-based program of restoration. Genesis II also operates an ecotourism facility and designs custom itineraries for its guests. Guests pay $75 per night, which covers costs for a naturalist guide, in addition to room and board. (Also see entry in Chapter 3, "Working in the Third World")

## Global Exchange (GX)

2017 Mission St., #303
San Francisco, CA 94110
(800) 497-1994, fax (415) 255-7498
gx-info@globalexchange.org
http://www.globalexchange.org

Global Exchange runs trips lasting 7-21 days with destinations such as Chile, Cuba, Guatemala, Haiti, Indonesia, Ireland, Israel/Palestine, Mexico, Nicaragua, the Philippines, Senegal, South Africa, Thailand and Vietnam. Participants meet with farmers, union representatives, church workers, human-rights and peace activists, indigenous groups, environmentalists, government officials, opposition leaders and representatives of other grassroots organizations. GX organizes election-monitoring and human rights delegations to countries experiencing social unrest.

GX also conducts tours in the U.S. to such locations as Native American reservations, the U.S.-Mexican border, and organic farms in California. Participants in these tours learn about poverty, homelessness, immigration and environmental issues.

Global Exchange provides a comprehensive follow-up program by which tour participants can continue their support of the grassroots efforts they witnessed. Some limited scholarships are available for low-income people and minorities. GX also organizes customized delegations for student groups, professional associations and community organizations.

## Lisle

433 W. Sterns Rd.

Temperance, MI 48182

(313) 847-7126, fax (419) 530-7719

mkinney@utnet.utoledo.edu

http://www.lisle.utoledo.edu

Lisle is a nonprofit, intercultural education organization. Since 1952, Lisle has sponsored educational programs in 11 states and 18 nations around the world. Its goal is to promote world peace and understanding through its program "units," which focus on a certain theme and last two to six weeks. Participants take part in the life and culture of their host communities, building close personal contacts through home-stays and/or volunteer work. Academic credit from the University of Toledo is available. Lisle programs are open to persons of all ages and backgrounds. Program sites vary from year to year.

## Marazul Tours

Tower Plaza

4100 Park Ave.

Weehawken, NJ 07087

(201) 319-9670 or (800) 223-5334; fax (201) 319-9009

marazul@igc.org

Marazul Tours is a travel agency that sponsors alternative tours to the Third World, particularly Central America, Haiti and Cuba. Tours to Cuba last for one to two weeks. Marazul Tours also make travel arrangements for many other alternative tour groups.

## Middle East Children's Alliance

2140 Shattuck Ave., #207

Berkeley, CA 94704

(510) 548-0542, fax (510) 548-0543

meca@igc.apc.org

The Middle East Children's Alliance is a national peace organization seeking a two-state solution for Palestine and Israel. The Alliance also raises funds for humanitarian aid (medical supplies, school books, food and clothing) for children in Iraq, the West Bank and Gaza. The Alliance also sponsors short-term delegations to Palestine and Israel. These delegates meet with Israeli peace activists and visit Palestinian cooperatives, refugee camps, health clinics and kindergartens in the West Bank and Gaza. Costs are $1000 not including airfare.

## Mobility International USA (MIUSA)

P.O. Box 10767

Eugene, OR 97440

(541) 343-1284 (voice/TDD); fax (541) 343-6812

miusa@igc.apc.org

MIUSA is a nonprofit organization dedicated to expanding equal opportunities for persons with disabilities in international educational exchange, leadership development, disability-rights training, travel and community service. MIUSA's international educational exchanges last from two to four weeks and are held throughout the year in the U.S. and abroad. Since 1981, MIUSA has coordinated exchanges with Bulgaria, China, Costa Rica, Germany, Great Britain, Italy, Japan, Mexico and Russia. Delegates live with families and participate in leadership training, workshops and seminars, adaptive recreation, language classes and community-service projects. Both able-bodied and disabled people are encouraged to apply. Fees vary according to the program. MIUSA also advises other exchange programs in the recruitment and accommodation of persons with disabilities, publishes resource books and a newsletter and produces videos. (Also see entry in Chapter 7.)

## Oceanic Society Expeditions (OSE)

Fort Mason Center

Building E, Suite 230

San Francisco, CA 94123-1394

(415) 441-1106 or (800) 326-7491; fax (415) 474-3395

OSE undertakes research to protect aquatic environments and promote environmental education. OSE works closely with indigenous populations, taking into account different cultural and economic conditions. Project locations include the Bahamas, Belize, the Peruvian Amazon, Surinam, Midway Atoll and Monterey Bay in California. Participants in OSE's expeditions become valuable members of the research team, actively contributing to its daily work. Tasks may include investigating the social and family structure, communication, distribution and abundance of free-ranging dolphins, primates, or manatees; monitoring sea-turtle nesting; assessing the impact of human activity on whales and dolphins; determining survival rates and movement patterns of seals and rehabilitating seal pups to the wild; conducting seabird population counts and monitoring chick hatchlings; or scuba-surveying tropical coral reefs and temperate submarine canyon ecosystems. No prior research or special skills are needed. Costs range from $290 to $2190, including travel expenses.

## Our Developing World (ODW)

13004 Paseo Presada
Saratoga, CA 95070
(408) 379-4431, fax (408) 376-0755
vic_ulmer@vval.com

Our Developing World is a nonprofit tax-exempt educational project designed to bring realities of the Third World and the richness of diverse cultures to North Americans. ODW has led study tours since 1975, helping travelers become more aware of development issues in the Third World. ODW currently offers one tour per year lasting two to three weeks, for a group of ten people; tour destinations are Central America in 1997, Southeast Asia in 1998 and South Africa in 1999. The cost of the tours ranges from $2200 to $3500, including airfare. ODW tours provide participants an opportunity to learn about health care, human rights, education campaigns, agrarian reform, and economic and social planning.

## Outward Bound USA

Route 9D
R2 Box 280
Garrison, NY 10524-9757
(914) 424-4000 or (800) 243-8520; fax (914) 424-4280
http://www.outwardbound.org

Outward Bound is the oldest and largest adventure-based educational organization in the U.S. Outward Bound uses challenging adventure and service activities to help its participants develop self-esteem, leadership skills, a sense of teamwork and respect for the environment. In addition to courses in the U.S., Outward Bound also organizes adventures in Costa Rica, Mexico, Nepal and Sweden. Courses occur year-round and range from four days to three months in length. The minimum age is 14 and there are special programs for persons over 55. Tuition is $495-$7795, which covers the cost of equipment, food and instruction. Other expenses include a $75 application fee, transportation to and from a pick-up location, personal clothing and footwear, a medical examination and possibly a fee for chartered transportation to the wilderness site. Scholarships based on financial need are available; some Outward Bound schools also offer low-interest loans.

## Pastors for Peace

610 W. 28th St.
Minneapolis, MN 55408

(612) 870-7121, fax (612) 870-7109
p4p@igc.apc.org

Pastors for Peace organizes national humanitarian aid caravans, human rights delegations, work brigades and study trips to Mexico, Central America and Cuba. Programs are designed to raise awareness throughout the U.S. about the impact of U.S. foreign policy on developing nations in this hemisphere and to provide opportunities for the establishment of "people-to-people" relationships across borders. Pastors for Peace organizes 20-25 study trips per year, lasting one to two weeks, to Mexico, Cuba and all five countries in Central America. Themes for study trips vary, but topics may include agriculture, education, ophthalmology and differents aspects of culture or religion. Each trip costs $500 to $1500 which may include partial travel expenses. (Also see entry in Chapter 3, "Working in the Third World")

## Pax World Service Tours
1111 16th St. NW, Suite 120
Washington, DC 20036
(202) 293-7290, fax (202) 293-7023
paxwldsvc@aol.com
http://members.aol.com/paxwldsvc

Pax World Service (formerly Pax World Foundation) was founded in 1971 as a nonprofit organization to advance sustainable development and promote peace and reconciliation in troubled regions throughout the world. Its programs support community-based initiatives, facilitate person-to-person contact across national and cultural boundaries, and encourage the development of global structures for enduring peace and security. Ten years ago, Pax World Service began conducting study- and working-tours to regions of conflict and need, placing participants in direct contact with the people and issues behind the news headlines. Whether the focus is on ecumenical travel, hands-on development and work tours, or fact-finding excursions, all trips provide a quality of travel experience that is unlike other, standard commercial tour packages. Trips include such destinations as Asia, the Middle East, Central and South America, the Caribbean and Eastern Europe. Tours generally last 10-12 days and vary in price.

## Plowshares Institute
P.O. Box 243
809 Hopmeadow St.
Simsbury, CT 06070

(860) 651-4304, fax (860) 651-4305

evansr@mstr.hgc.edu

Plowshares Institute is a nonprofit organization in the service of the Church, promoting justice and peace in the world community. Plowshares's mission includes service, education, and research in Africa, Asia, Latin America, Eastern Europe and the United States. It emphasizes community conflict-resolution; awareness education for the privileged; and partnership programs in education, health and development in the developing world. Plowshares offers traveling seminars lasting two to three weeks, in which participants are hosted by local religious, political, civic, business, cultural and grassroots leaders. Upcoming seminars have been scheduled in South Africa, Hong Kong and China, Brazil and Indonesia. Participants will have opportunities to visit individuals in their homes and develop close personal contacts. As much as possible, the group will gather every evening for a period of sharing, worship and a discussion of issues led by experienced staff or hosts. The cost (approximately $3500) includes tuition, room and board and travel from New York or the West Coast.

## Third World Opportunities (TWO)

1363 Somermont Dr.

El Cajon, CA 92021

(619) 449-9381

TWO offers short-term experiences that introduce its participants to the realities of hunger, poverty and border issues. Although their programs may be brief in length, TWO emphasizes long-range development rather than short-term, charity-type projects.

Awareness experiences lasting one day or one weekend are located in Tijuana and Tecate, Mexico. These trips are open to people of all ages and cost $20 per day. TWO (with Habitat for Humanity) also offers short-term work opportunities with the "Servant Event," a straw-bale house-building project located in Tecate and Tijuana, lasting one week. Participants in the event must be at least 15 years old. The cost is $200 for six days, not including transportation.

## Tour de Caña Bicycle Tours

P.O. Box 7293

Philadelphia, PA 19101

(215) 222-1253, fax (215) 222-0221

tourdecana@igc.apc.org

Tour de Caña organizes tours between December and April annually, allowing cyclists to experience different cultures firsthand. Tours are generally limited to 12 people. Tour sites include Belize, Honduras, Quintana Roo in Mexico and (for journalists only) Cuba. A typical seven-day tour in Mexico costs $400, not including airfare, with an average cycling distance of 30 miles per day. Tours in the Caribbean may also use a boat to carry equipment and supplies.

## US Servas

11 John St., Suite 407
New York, NY 10038-4009
(212) 267-0252, fax (212) 267-0292
usservas@igc.apc.org

US Servas does not offer tours, but provides a unique service to individual travelers by linking them with host families. The program is designed to facilitate deeper, more personal contacts among people of diverse cultures. By participating in a two-night visit, host and traveler share their lives, interests, and concerns about social and international issues. In addition to hosts throughout the U.S. and Western Europe, Servas also has members in Africa, Asia, Latin America, Eastern Europe and the former Soviet Union. Participants must be at least 18 years old.

## Wisconsin Coordinating Council on Nicaragua (WCCN)

P.O. Box 1534
Madison, WI 53701
(608) 257-7230, fax (608) 257-7904
wccn@igc.apc.org

WCCN is a nonprofit, tax-exempt educational organization that builds on the historic sister-state relationship between Wisconsin and Nicaragua; its primary purpose is to work with Nicaraguans to promote peace and justice. WCCN offers one to two opportunities per year for members and other interested persons to participate in study tours to Nicaragua lasting seven to ten days. Each tour relates to WCCN's primary projects and addresses salient issues in Nicaraguan and U.S. society. For example, WCCN sponsors a tour every June that focuses on the Women's Empowerment Project. WCCN also offers a tour that explores economic, environmental and/or social issues. Costs depend upon the length and type of activities in a given tour and start at $800 per person, not including airfare. This fee includes three meals per day, lodging, in-country transportation, interpretation/translation and pre-trip materials.

## Youth For Understanding International Exchange (YFU)

Program Information Office
3501 Newark St. NW
Washington, DC 20016-3199
(202) 895-1122 or (800) TEENAGE (833-6243); fax (202) 895-1104
pio@yfu.org

The YFU International Exchange is an organization promoting international understanding and world peace through student-exchange programs for high-school students, ages 14-19. YFU students are hosted by families for periods lasting from a single summer up to an entire academic year. YFU also offers a program called Sport For Understanding in which students (led by volunteer coaches) travel overseas for three to four weeks, practicing and competing as part of a team in nearly a dozen sports. Program placements are offered in dozens of countries, including Argentina, Brazil, Chile, Ecuador, Mexico, Russia, Slovakia, South Korea, Uruguay and Venezuela.

In most cases, no previous language study is required. Summer programs require that applicants have a GPA of 2.0 or better. Fees for YFU summer programs start at $2440. The cost for the Sport For Understanding program ranges from $2800 to $3100. Fees cover round-trip international travel and visa assistance, domestic travel, cultural and educational activities, placement with and screening of host families, orientation and handbooks, and emergency assistance.

7
GETTING
MORE
INFORMATION

Part of your preparation for going overseas should be to immerse yourself in books, audiovisual materials and other resources that deal with development and intercultural issues.

Global Exchange, our organization, has excellent educational resources on the Third World. We distribute a wide range of books, pamphlets, audio tapes, documentary videos, and we provide dynamic speakers on a range of contemporary issues. For a list of our resources call (800) 497-1994.

An excellent resource is the *Third World Resource Directories,* by Thomas Fenton and Mary Heffron (Orbis Books, Maryknoll, NY). They offer several different directories with lists of organizations, films, videos and other resources on development issues. Directories are available on Asia, the Middle East, women in the Third World, human rights, food and agribusiness, transnational corporations and labor, and Third World struggles for peace with justice. Fenton and Heffron have also written the 800-page *Third World Resource Directory 1994-1995* (Orbis Books, Maryknoll, NY) which covers all regions of the Third World, the aforementioned topics and much more. Another directory, *Africa: Africa World Press Guide to Educational Resources from and about Africa*, is being published by Africa World Press in April 1997. These are all available from WorldViews (formerly Third World Resources) at 464 19th St., Oakland, CA 94612; (510) 835-4692.

Another source of information on development issues is the Institute for Food and Development Policy/Food First. Their books include *Food First* and *World Hunger: 12 Myths*. Write for a catalog to Food First Books at 398 60th St., Oakland, CA 94609; or call (510) 654-4400.

A good resource on environmental volunteer work is the Traveler's Earth Repair Network (TERN), Friends of the Trees Society, P.O. Box 4469, Bellingham, WA 98227; (360) 738-4972, fax (360) 738-4972. TERN is a database project of Friends of the Trees Society that lists over 3000 addresses of organizations from over 100 countries which are involved in sustainable forestry, sustainable agriculture, permaculture, restoration and environmental issues. Project locations are in Africa, Asia, Latin America, Eastern Europe and the former Soviet Union. It also has over 200 host contacts which offer living arrangements and opportunities for hands-on involvement. TERN's fee for travelers is $50.

A terrific source of information on adapting to foreign cultures is Intercultural Press, P.O. Box 700, Yarmouth, ME 04096; (207) 846-5168, fax (207) 846-5181. It carries a full line of books and videos dealing with cross-cultural issues, including many country-specific titles. Titles include *The Art of Crossing Cultures* (1990), *The Art of Coming Home* (1997), *On Being Foreign: Culture Shock in Short Fiction* (1986), and *Survival Kit for Overseas Living* (3rd ed., 1996).

For information on the negative impact of tourism in the Third World, contact the Center for Responsible Tourism, P.O. Box 827, San Anselmo, CA 94979; (415) 258-6594, fax (415) 258-1608. Its present research focus is the environment and human rights. The Center offers resources, including its quarterly newsletter, *Responsible Travelling*, to individuals and groups interested in responsible tourism. It also distributes *Contours,* the quarterly newsletter of the Ecumenical Coalition on Third World Tourism.

For low-cost films, slide shows and videos on Third World issues, contact the AFSC Film Library at 2161 Massachusetts Ave., Cambridge, MA 02140, (617) 497-5273, and Maryknoll Audiovisual Resources in Maryknoll, NY 10545.

A great source of information on U.S. foreign relations with the Third World is the Interhemispheric Resource Center at P.O. Box 4506, Albuquerque, NM 87196; (505) 842-8288. It produces books, policy reports, audiovisual materials and a quarterly bulletin. Also try the Resource Center of the Americas, 317 17th Ave. SE, Minneapolis, MN 55414-2077; (612) 627-9445, fax (612) 627-9450. It produces and distributes *Central America: The Month in Review* and curriculum materials on Mexico, Guatemala, El Salvador and the global economy.

For more information on organizations and workcamp opportunities in other countries, contact the Coordinating Committee for International Voluntary Service (CCIVS), UNESCO, 1 rue Miollis, 75732 Paris Cedex 15, France; (33-1) 45-68-27-31, ccivs@zcc.net

CCIVS is an international, nongovernmental organization that coordinates voluntary service and workcamp activities worldwide. Members include 142 organizations in over 100 countries, half of which are in Africa, Asia and Latin America. CCIVS also has at their disposal directories of workcamp organizations (one for Africa and Asia, another for Europe and North America), each costing $4, including postage costs.

## Publications on Working in the Third World, U.S. and Canada

*Academic Year Abroad* (1996-1997, published annually) describes over 2300 semester and academic-year programs offered by U.S. and foreign universities, language schools and private organizations. Institute of International Education Distribution Center, P.O. Box 371, Annapolis Junction, MD 20701; (301) 617-7804 or (800) 445-0443. Cost: $42.95, plus $4 s/h.

*After Latin American Studies: A Guide to Employment for Latin Americanists,* by Alan Adelman (1995) provides information on internships, grants and employment in Latin America. Latin America Studies, 4E04 Forbes Quadrangle, University of Pittsburgh, Pittsburgh, PA 15260; (412) 648-7392. Cost: $10.

*Archaeological Fieldwork Opportunities Bulletin* (published annually) lists projects around the world in need of volunteers. Archaeological Institute of America (AIA), distributed by Kendall-Hunt Publishers, Order Dept., 4050 Westmark Dr., P.O. Box 1840, Dubuque, IA 52004; (800) 228-0810. Cost: $9 (for members), $11 (nonmembers) plus $4 s/h.

Archaeology Abroad is an organization which publishes three bulletins each year. 31-34 Gordon Square, London WC1H OPY, England.

*Career Opportunities in International Development in Washington, DC* (1994). Overseas Development Network, 333 Valencia St., Suite 330, San Francisco, CA 94103; (415) 431-4204. Cost: $6 (for students), $9 (individuals), $12 (institutions).

*Careers in International Affairs,* 6th ed., edited by Gerhard F. Sheehan (1996). School of Foreign Service, Georgetown University, Georgetown, distributed by Career Guide, P.O. Box 4866, Hampden Station, Baltimore, MD 21211-4866; (800) 246-9606. Cost: $17.95 plus $3.50 s/h.

*Community Jobs: The National Employment Newspaper for the Non-Profit Sector* (published monthly). ACCESS, 1001 Connecticut Ave. NW, Suite 838, Washington, DC 20036; (202) 785-4233. Cost: $25 (for three months), $39 (six months), $69 (full year).

*Connections: A Directory of Lay Volunteer Service Opportunities* (1996) is a listing of over 100 volunteer positions at home and overseas. St. Vincent Pallotti Center, P.O. Box 893, Cardinal Station, Washington, DC 20064; (202) 529-3330. Cost: free.

*Crossing Borders: A Resource on U.S.-Mexico Cross Cultural Exchange Programs,* by Denise Plechaty-Fallon (1993). Mobility International USA, P.O. Box 10767, Eugene, OR 97440; (541) 343-1284 (voice/TDD). Cost: $12 (for members), $14 (nonmembers) plus s/h.

*Development Opportunities Catalog* (1993, with 1996 update) is a guide to national and international volunteer work and employment opportunities at U.S. organizations working in international development. Overseas Development Network, 333 Valencia St., Suite 330, San Francisco, CA 94103; (415) 431-4204. Cost: $7 (for students), $10 (individuals), $15 (institutions).

*DevelopNet News* is a monthly electronic newsletter. Volunteers in Technical Assistance (VITA), 1600 Wilson Blvd., Suite 500, Arlington, VA 22209; (703) 276-1800, fax (703) 243-1865. To subscribe, send the following message to listserv@american.edu: "sub dnn-l <first name> <last name>."

*Directory of International Internships: A World of Opportunities,* compiled and edited by Charles Gliozzo, Vernicka K. Lupow, Bob Dije and Adela Peña (1990). Career Services and Placement, 113 Student Services Bldg., Michigan State University, East Lansing, MI 48824; (517) 355-9510 ext. 371. Cost: $25 including s/h.

*Directory of Jobs and Careers Abroad,* 9th ed., by Alex Lipinski (1997). Vacation Work, distributed by Peterson's Guides, P.O. Box 2123, Princeton, NJ 08543-2123; (800) 338-3282. Cost: $16.95 plus s/h. *Directory of Overseas Summer Jobs,* by David Woodworth. Vacation Work, distributed by Peterson's Guides, P.O. Box 2123, Princeton, NJ 08543-2123; (800) 338-3282. Cost: $15.95 plus $4.75 s/h.

*Directory of U.S.-Based Agencies Involved in International Health Assistance* (1997) includes information on over 750 U.S. agencies with Third World programs in health, nutrition and population. National Council for International Health (NCIH), 1701 K St. NW, Suite 600, Washington, DC 20006-1503; (202) 833-5900. Cost: $30 (for members), $60 (nonmembers) plus s/h.

*Going Places* (1997) is a booklet listing opportunities to work with nonprofit social organizations in the U.S. and abroad. National Student Campaign Against Hunger and Homelessness, 11965 Venice Blvd., Suite 408, Los Angeles, CA 90066; (310) 397-5270, ext. 324. Cost: $6.25.

*A Guide to Careers in World Affairs* by Foreign Policy Association (1993) FPA, 470 Park Avenue South, 2nd Floor, New York, NY 10016 (212) 481-8100 ext. 226 or (800) 477-5836. Cost $14.95.

*A Handbook for Creating Your Own Internship in International Development* has information on how to get internships in international development. Overseas Development Network, 333 Valencia St., #330, San Francisco, CA 94103; (415) 431-4204. Cost: $7.95.

*How to Find an Overseas Job with the U.S. Government,* by Will Cantrell and Francine Modderno (1992). Worldwise Books, P.O. Box 3030, Oakton, VA 22124; (703) 620-1972. Cost: $28.95 including s/h.

*How to Get a Job in the Pacific Rim* (1993). Surrey Books, 230 E. Ohio St., Suite 120, Chicago, IL 60611; (800) 326-4430. Cost: $17.95.

*International Agriculture, A World of Opportunities,* by Philip Warnken, Eric Scherff and Thomas Love (1990) includes international opportunities for many agricultural specialists. Extension Publications, University of Missouri, 2800 Maguire Blvd., Columbia, MO 65211; (573) 882-2792. Cost: $7.00 plus $1 s/h.

*International Directory for Youth Internships* (1992). The Apex Press, 777 United Nations Plaza, Suite 3C, New York, NY 10017, (800) 316-APEX.

*International Career Employment Opportunities* (published biweekly) lists positions in foreign affairs and subjects such as international trade, finance, development and education. The Carlyle Company, Route 2, Box 305, Stanardsville, VA 22973, (804) 985-6444, fax (804) 985-6828. Cost: $29 (for four issues).

*The International Directory of Volunteer Work,* by David Woodworth (1996, revised every three years). Vacation Work, distributed by Peterson's Guides, P.O. Box 2123, Princeton, NJ 08543-2123; (800) 338-3282. Cost: $15.95 plus $4.75 s/h.

*International Employment Hotline,* edited by Will Cantrell (published monthly). Worldwise Books, P.O. Box 3030, Oakton, VA 22124; (703) 620-1972. Cost: $39 (per year).

*International Internships and Volunteer Programs,* by Will Cantrell and Francine Modderno (1992). Worldwise Books, P.O. Box 3030, Oakton, VA 22124; (703) 620-1972. Cost: $18.95 including s/h.

*International Workcamp Directory* (revised every April). Service Civil International-International Voluntary Service (SCI-IVS), 5474 Walnut Level Rd., Crozet, VA 22932; (804) 823-1826, fax (804) 823-5027. Cost: $5.00.

*International Workcamp Directory* (revised every April) lists hundreds of opportunities for young people to work together on short-term projects (usually during the summer months) in Africa, Asia, Australia, Latin America, Eastern and Western Europe and the former Soviet Union. Volunteers for Peace, 43 Tiffany Rd., Belmont, VT 05730-0202; (802) 259-2759, fax (802) 259-2922. Cost: $12.00.

*Internships,* edited by Kathryn Walden (1997, published annually). Peterson's Guides, P.O. Box 2123, Princeton, NJ 08543-2123; (800) 338-3282. Cost: $24.95 plus $5.75 s/h.

*Member Profiles* is a directory of the 143 international relief and development agencies which are members of InterAction and have programs abroad. InterAction, 1717 Massachusetts Ave. NW, Suite 801, Washington, DC 20036; (202) 667-8227. Cost: $43 including s/h.

*Monday Developments* (published biweekly) is a newsletter listing job opportunities with large international relief and development agencies. InterAction, 1717 Massachusetts Ave. NW, Suite 801, Washington, DC 20036; (202) 667-8227. Cost: $4 (per copy).

*Opportunities in Africa.* The African-American Institute, 380 Lexington, New York, NY 10168; (212) 949-5666. Cost: $5 including s/h.

*Opportunities in Grassroots Development in California* (1994, with 1996 update). Overseas Development Network, 333 Valencia St., Suite 330, San Francisco, CA 94103; (415) 431-4204. Cost: $7 (for students), $10 (individuals), $15 (institutions).

*Opportunities in International Development in New England* (1993, with 1996 update). Overseas Development Network, 333 Valencia St., Suite 330, San Francisco, CA 94103; (415) 431-4204. Cost: $7 (for students), $10 (individuals), $15 (institutions).

Options is a professional recruitment and referral service linking doctors, nurses and other health care professionals with programs, medical missions, hospitals and clinics in the U.S. and abroad. The $25 membership fee covers referral service and subscription to a bimonthly newsletter listing current volunteer opportunities. Project Concern International, 3550 Afton Rd., San Diego, CA 92123; (619) 279-9690, fax (619) 694-0294.

The Quaker Information Center provides information on numerous Friends-related opportunities around the world. It also publishes a comprehensive list of international and domestic, Quaker and non-Quaker, short-, medium- and long-term volunteer service opportunities. Quaker Information Center, 1501 Cherry St., Philadelphia, PA 19102; (215) 241-7024, fax (215) 567-2096.

*The Response: Lay Volunteer Mission Opportunities Directory.* Catholic Network of Volunteer Service, 4121 Harewood Rd. NE, Washington, DC 20017; (800) 543-5046. Cost: free (donations accepted).

*Schools Abroad of Interest to Americans* (1991-92) lists 800 elementary and secondary schools enrolling American and English-speaking students in 130 countries. Porter Sargent Publishers, 11 Beacon St., Suite 1400, Boston, MA 02108; (617) 523-1670. Cost: $35 plus s/h.

*Teaching English Abroad,* by Susan Griffith (1996, revised every three years). Vacation Work, distributed by Peterson's Guides, P.O. Box 2123, Princeton, NJ 08543-2123; (800) 338-3282. Cost: $16.95 plus $4.75 s/h.

*Teaching Overseas K-12.* International Resource Guides, Transitions Abroad, P.O. Box 1300, Amherst, MA 01004; (800) 293-0373. Cost: $5.

*Transitions Abroad* (published bimonthly) is a magazine listing up-to-date international study, travel, work and living opportunities. Each July/August issue features the "Overseas Travel Planner." Transitions Abroad, P.O. Box 1300, Amherst, MA 01004; (800) 293-0373. Cost: $24.95 (per year).

*Volunteer! The Comprehensive Guide to Voluntary Service in the U.S. and Abroad,* 5th ed., edited by Richard Christiano (1994-1995, published biannually). Council of Religious Volunteer Agencies (CRVA) and the Council on International Educational Exchange, distributed by CIEE, 205 E. 42nd St., New York, NY 10017; (212) 822-2600 or (800) 349-2433. Cost: $12.95 plus $1.50 s/h.

*Work, Study, Travel Abroad: The Whole World Handbook,* edited by Del Franz and Lazaro Hernandez (1994-1995). St. Martin's Press, also distributed by the Council on International Educational Exchange, 205 E. 42nd St., New York, NY 10017; (800) 349-2433. Cost: $6.95 plus postage.

*Work Your Way Around the World,* by Susan Griffith (1996). Vacation Work, from Peterson's Guides, P.O. Box 2123, Princeton, NJ 08543-2123; (800) 338-3282. Cost: $17.95 plus $4.75 s/h.

*Working Holidays* (1996, published annually). Institute of International Education Distribution Center, P.O. Box 371, Annapolis Junction, MD 20701; (301) 617-7804 or (800) 445-0443. Cost: $18.95 plus $2 s/h

*A World of Options for the 90's: A Guide to International Educational Exchange, Community Service and Travel for Persons with Disabilities,* by Susan Sygall, edited by Christa Lewis (1996). Mobility International USA, P.O. Box 10767, Eugene, OR 97440; (541) 343-1284 (voice/TDD). Cost: $14 (for members), $16 (nonmembers) plus s/h.

*Writing Jobs Abroad.* International Resource Guides, Transitions Abroad, P.O. Box 1300, Amherst, MA 01004; (800) 293-0373. Cost: $5.

## Publications on Study, Travel and Tourism in the Third World

*Academic Year Abroad* (1996-1997, published annually) describes over 2300 programs offered by U.S. and foreign universities, language schools and private organizations. Institute of International Education Distribution Center, P.O. Box 371, Annapolis Junction, MD 20701; (301) 617-7804 or (800) 445-0443. Cost: $42.95 plus $4 s/h.

*Advisory List of International Educational Travel and Exchange Programs* (published annually) describes international educational travel and exchange organizations at the high-school level that comply with CSIET standards. Council on Standards for International Educational Travel (CSIET), 3 Loudoun St. SE, Leesburg, VA 20175; (703) 771-2040, fax (703) 771-2046.

*Alternative Travel Directory* (revised every January). This is one of most comprehensive and reliable resources available. Transitions Abroad, P.O. Box 1300, Amherst, MA 01004; (800) 293-0373. Cost: $19.95 plus s/h. *Basic Facts on Study Abroad* (1990). Institute of International Education Distribution Center, P.O. Box 371, Annapolis Junction, MD 20701; (301) 617-7804 or (800) 445-0443. Cost: free.

*Break Away SiteBank Catalog* lists alternative school-break programs with volunteer work-study opportunities in Latin America, the Caribbean and the U.S. Break Away: The Alternative Break Connection, P.O. 6026, Station B, Nashville, TN 37235; (615) 343-0385, ext. 2; fax (615) 343-3255.

*Calendar of Opportunities for Peace Teams and Short-Term Delegations* lists peace teams sponsored by organizations involved in accompaniment, documentation of human rights abuses, advocacy, rapid-response networks and public education on human rights. Michigan Faith and Resistance Peace Team (MPT), 1516 Jerome St., Lansing, MI 48912; (517) 484-3178.

*Contours (Concern for Tourism Magazine)* and *Alternative Tourism: A Resource Book*. Ecumenical Coalition on Third World Tourism (ECTWT), P.O. Box 24, Chorakhebua, Bangkok 10230, Thailand.

*El Planeta Platica: Eco Travels in Latin America* (published quarterly) is a newsletter featuring a constantly-updated list of Spanish schools in Latin America, some of which offer short- and long-term volunteer opportunities. Directory of Latin American Spanish Language Schools (attn: Ron Mader), P.O. Box 1044, Austin, TX 78767, ron@versa.com http://www.planeta.com/mader/schools/schoolist

*The High School Student's Guide to Study, Travel and Adventure Abroad,* edited by Richard Christiano (1995). Council on International Educational Exchange, 205 E. 42nd St., New York, NY 10017; (212) 822-2600 or (800) 349-2433. Cost: $6.95 plus s/h.

*Indochina Interchange* (published quarterly) is a publication listing trips to the region organized by NGOs and academic programs operating in Southeast Asia. U.S.-Indochina Reconciliation Project (USIRP), 25 W. 45th St., #1201, New York, NY 10036; (212) 764-3925, fax (212) 764-3896.

*The ISS Directory of Overseas Schools* (1996, published annually).

International Schools Services (ISS), distributed by Peterson's Guides, P.O. Box 2123, Princeton, NJ 08543; (800) 338-3282. Cost: $34.95 plus s/h.

*Over the Rainbow* (published quarterly) is a newsletter with information and resources pertaining to international travel for people with disabilities. Mobility International USA, P.O. Box 10767, Eugene, OR 97440; (541) 343-1284 (voice/TDD). Cost: $25 (membership fee including one-year subscription) $15 (one-year subscription for nonmembers).

*Student Travels Magazine* (revised every spring and fall) includes traveling tips, and programs and services offered by CIEE and other groups. Council on International Educational Exchange, 205 E. 42nd St., New York, NY 10017; (212) 822-2600 or (800) 349-2433. Cost: free.

*Study Abroad: A Guide for Men and Women* (1996). Institute of International Education Distribution Center, P.O. Box 371, Annapolis Junction, MD 20701; (301) 617-7804 or (800) 445-0443. Cost: free.

*Study Tours,* by Vicky Busch (1996). Public Affairs Department, Athabasca University, Box 10000, Athabasca, Alberta T9S 1A1, Canada; (403) 675-6109. Cost: Can$24.02 including s/h.

*Trans-Cultural Study Guide* (1987). Volunteers in Asia, P.O. Box 4543, Stanford, CA 94309; (415) 723-3228. Cost: $7.95 plus s/h.

*Travel Programs in Central America.* Interfaith Task Force on Central America, P.O. Box 3843, La Mesa, CA 91944; (619) 687-7875. Cost: $8.

*Vacation Study Abroad: A Complete Guide* (1996) lists 1800 summer and short-term programs worldwide. Institute of International Education Distribution Center, P.O. Box 371, Annapolis Junction, MD 20701; (301) 617-7804 or (800) 445-0443. Cost: $36.95 plus $4 s/h.

*Volunteer Vacations: A Directory of Short Term Adventures That Will Benefit You... and Others,* 5th ed., by Bill McMillon (1995). Chicago Review Press, Inc., 814 N. Franklin St., Chicago, IL 60610; (312) 337-0747. Cost: $13.95 plus s/h.

*Work, Study, Travel Abroad: The Whole World Handbook,* edited by Del Franz and Lazaro Hernandez (1994-1995). St. Martin's Press, also from the Council on International Educational Exchange, 205 E. 42nd St., New York, NY 10017; (212) 822-2600 or (800) 349-2433. Cost: $6.95 plus s/h.

*A World of Options for the 90's: A Guide to International Educational Exchange, Community Service and Travel for Persons with Disabilities,* by Susan Sygall, edited by Christa Lewis (1996). Mobility International USA, P.O. Box 10767, Eugene, OR 97440; (541) 343-1284 (voice/TDD). Cost: $14 (for members), $16 (nonmembers) plus s/h.

*You Want to Go Where? A Guide to China,* by Evelyn Anderton and Susan Sygall (1990). Mobility International USA, P.O. Box 10767, Eugene, OR 97440; (541) 343-1284 (voice/TDD). Cost: $7.95 (for members), $8.95 (nonmembers) plus s/h.

**Fundraising Resources**
*Directory of Financial Aids for International Activities* (1985). Office of International Activities, University of Minnesota.

*Financial Resources for International Study* (1996). Institute of International Education Distribution Center, P.O. Box 371, Annapolis Junction, MD 20701; (301) 617-7804 or (800) 445-0443.

*Grants for Graduates in Post-Doctoral Studies* (1994). Peterson's Guides, P.O. Box 2123, Princeton, NJ 08543-2123; (800) 338-3282. Cost: $89.95 plus s/h.

*International Studies Funding and Resources Book.* (1990) The Apex Press, 777 United Nations Plaza, Suite 3C, New York, NY 10017; (800) 316-APEX.

# Index

# GLOBAL EXCHANGE

*Global Exchange works to create more justice and economic opportunity in the world. The heart of our work is the involvement of thousands of supporters around the country.*

*When you become a member of GX you get:*
- our quarterly newsletter and Action Alerts;
- regular updates on our material aid campaigns and our support for development projects;
- priority on our Reality Tours to dozens of foreign countries and domestic destinations;
- a 10 percent discount on our educational materials and crafts sold at our third world craft stores;
- plus, you get connected to a growing global network of concerned citizens working to transform the world from the bottom up.

*Please use the coupon below to join Global Exchange today.*

✂ — — — — — — — — — — — — — — — — — — — — —

**YES**, I want to support Global Exchange's efforts to build people-to-people ties. Enclosed is my tax-deductible membership contribution.

___ $100 ___$50 ___$35 ___other

Name_____

Address_____

City_____ State____ Zip_____

Phone_____

## GLOBAL EXCHANGE

2017 Mission Street, Suite 303, San Francisco, CA 94110
(415) 255-7296, FAX (415) 255-7498
email: gx-info@globalexchange.org